בס"ד

Yosif & Eugenia Varenboud
Tzvi & Francis Balofsky
Elena & Slava Kassimov
Yuri Kofman & Dina Akilov
Rabbi Yoseph & Chiena Zaltzman
Rabbi Shmuel & Esther Neft
Roman & Polina Spektor
Moshe Zalipski
Jamie Domb
Rafael & Malka Tchetyshov
Rishon & Batel Talkar

# Australian Encounters

*An attorney shares
firsthand stories of the
Lubavitcher Rebbe*

ROBERT KREMNIZER

SIMCHA
PRESS

**Australian Encounters**

Published and Copyrighted © 2021
*Second Printing—August 2023*
by
**Simcha Press**

Orders:
291 Kingston Avenue / Brooklyn, New York 11213
(718) 778-0226 / Fax: (718) 778-4148
www.kehot.com

All rights reserved. No part of this publication may be reproduced, stored in a retrieval system, or transmitted in any form or by any means, electronic, mechanical, photocopying, recording, or otherwise, without prior permission from the copyright holder.

ISBN 978-0-8266-0829-1

*Printed in Türkiye*

# Read this first

There is a fascinating exchange of letters between the Lubavitcher Rebbe and his father-in-law, the Previous Lubavitcher Rebbe, on the subject of miracles.

The tradition in Chabad, explains the Previous Rebbe, is that miracles, especially those emanating from a Rebbe, are viewed with disdain. There are many and deep reasons for this, and this is an inappropriate forum to discuss them. Suffice it to say that our Rebbe, obviously with great respect, questions this.

His point is that after the decimation of our nation, the task of bringing Jews back to observance of Torah and *mitzvot* is paramount. People of little education may better respond to the many miracles than more difficult introductory pathways. The value of these miracles therefore deserves highlighting.

My generation saw an incredible number of miracles from the Rebbe, and there is hardly a Chabad family that does not have their own cache of them. Sadly, however, due to what is surely eager zeal to impress others about the Rebbe, some may be exaggerated. This is a terrible shame, because the Rebbe does not need any form of packaging, and any slight crack in the absolute truth about him must ultimately be destructive.

My family, like so many others, has a trove of miracles.

This book is a response to my children and grandchildren, who have pressed me to record them. Their argument is that my generation is obligated to share these involvements with the Rebbe with subsequent generations.

I am doing so scrupulously, careful not to exaggerate or color any of them. I am deliberately not including any stories that took place with other people—even good friends whom I trust unreservedly about this—because I want to be able to present these stories as the absolute pristine truth. The only rider to this is the names used. Except for my teachers and family, all names have been changed for obvious reasons.

I can therefore assure any reader that these stories happened exactly as presented— often witnessed by others who can verify them.

# The New Chabad House
*chapter 1*

**ONE**

In the early 1980s, my legal work involved expertise in two uncommon and extremely lucrative areas. One of them was legal tax sheltering. The other was exploiting a loophole in the Australian Reserve Bank's prohibition against foreign nationals buying Australian real estate. Both methodologies were, of course, perfectly legal. My knowledge in both areas came from a law school friend who was much cleverer than I and was happy to share what he had learned because he made considerable fees from my involvement.

This story came as a result of my work in both areas.

## Australian Encounters

## TWO

I arranged a creative tax shelter for an asset-rich but cash-poor entrepreneur who had made a fortune from women's handbags. He promised me an apartment in Surfers Paradise (in Gold Coast, Queensland) if I could perform. I had never had an offer for fees like that, so you can imagine that I was keenly motivated. Fortunately, the exercise was a success, and when the client received clearance from the ATO (Australian Taxation Office), he kept his side of the bargain. My wife, Ann, and I suddenly became the owners of an apartment in Australia's premier holiday location. The value of the apartment was $75,000—a considerable sum at the time.

A week later we took a flight to inspect our new holiday home. Upon arriving at the building, we were ushered in by an agent bursting with enthusiasm. She offered to rent it out as part of their time-share management business and would guarantee us three weeks a year in the apartment. She was so proud of herself. We had not been inside for more than twenty seconds when Ann's face told me how completely mistaken the agent was. The property faced the wrong way, the apartment was on a floor that was too low for a decent view, the bathroom was awful, the kitchen had to be replaced, and so on. Ann gave me a firm look and then sweetly gave instructions to the agent to sell the property immediately.

On the plane back to our home in Sydney, Ann explained (rightfully) how much better our position would be if we used the money from that apartment to invest in local real estate. Furthermore, instead of one apartment, we could buy a small building with multiple apartments if we got a conservative mortgage. Thankfully, I boast the good sense to have listened to her.

A short time later, she found a building with four apartments for about $200,000. We contributed the $75,000 gained from the sale of the unit in Surfers Paradise, and I arranged a mortgage for $125,000. We rented them out to four separate tenants, and my wife and I were satisfied with the outcome.

### THREE

A couple of years before this purchase, a man named David James made an appointment with me for a consultation. He was a New Zealander, sleekly handsome, carefully dressed in expensive clothes, and bearing an incessant smile that flashed blindingly white teeth.

He was charming, disarmingly sincere, and very polite throughout our meeting.

His story was that he was a property developer who, having outgrown his home country of New Zealand, wanted to build an empire in Australia. The problem was that foreign nationals could not buy Australian real estate. I had been recommended to him as someone who had the expertise to facilitate his plans notwithstanding the apparent prohibition.

He understood, he continued, how valuable my contribution would be, and he accepted that the fees would be expensive. However, as the adventure in Australia was just beginning, it was better business to utilize his cash for the acquisition and development of property, so he proposed a different form of payment. I was to receive a percentage of all net profits from the sales of all ventures in Australia for the first five years of this endeavor. When he showed me his business plan, this amount far exceeded the fee I had expected to charge. Additionally, my office would do all the legal work for the site acquisitions, funding, and ultimate sale of the newly-built offices or apartments. The reader can understand that I was delighted with the arrangement.

I went to work. I won't go into the details, but the methodology required a specific kind of company to be formed with a local shareholder (me) and then a discretionary trust in partnership with a blind trust—all carefully tooled to be fully compliant.

A few months later, we received government approval, and James danced into my office with an expensive bottle of single malt, which he insisted should be shared with the entire staff.

And then he disappeared.

I saw no site acquisitions; no funding documentation; no sales. I saw no profit share, and, indeed, no David James.

## FOUR

Fast forward to a couple of weeks after we had closed

*chapter 1*

on the building purchase mentioned above; I went to *shul*, as usual.

This was in the early '80s, in times of more primitive technology. When the Lubavitcher Rebbe spoke on weekdays, his voice was directed via microphone to a telephone bank located in the central Chabad *shul* at 770 Eastern Parkway in Brooklyn. From there it was broadcast to many locations via telephone hookup, which could be accessed by dialing in to a particular phone number. People would gather at their local *shuls* in the US and abroad, where the other end of the designated telephone was set before another microphone amplified to a speaker on the wall. It was thus possible to communally hear the Rebbe speak "live."

Such an arrangement existed in the Yeshiva Centre in Sydney. As the Rebbe's voice came over the microphone in Yiddish, a young rabbi translated for the crowd.

That morning, after *davening*, I was in the audience. Of course, there was total silence other than the two voices, with everyone straining to listen and concentrate.

The Rebbe spoke with passion about the need for new entities to be created and called "Chabad Houses." These Chabad Houses were to be islands of spirituality; places where Jews, traveling or otherwise, could find familiar surroundings, opportunities to worship, opportunities to learn, and places to eat kosher meals. I venture to say there were few people listening to that hookup globally who dreamed that twenty-five years later the number of Chabad Houses worldwide would exceed 4,500!

During his talk, the Rebbe anticipated the predictable financial question. Where would the money come from for such Chabad Houses? During his calling on his followers to provide the money, the Rebbe used a bewildering expression. He enjoined everyone listening to "*trust me in this*," paraphrasing from a verse in which G-d promises to repay those who take care of the poor.

When I went home for breakfast, I was on fire. The Rebbe's passion was totally engulfing. At the first break in the family static, I called Ann into a separate room, closed the door, and tried as best as I could to repeat the impassioned address. I then broke the suggestion to her.

"How would you feel about donating one of the new units as a Chabad House?"

I held my breath and looked out the window.

"Fine."

"Fine?! Are you sure?" I gasped.

"If you want to, I want to," she said simply.

I almost ran to the phone and called my close friend, Rabbi Feldman, who was in charge of the Yeshiva Centre and had been present at the hookup. He also knew about our acquisition of the apartments.

Excitedly, I told him what an impression the Rebbe had made on me and how my wife and I both wanted to participate in this endeavor. Then I announced in triumph: "We want to donate one of the units as a Chabad House!"

There was silence. Then, gently but regretfully, Rabbi Feldman said, "What can I do with one unit? If it were the whole building that would be different. Then it could work. But one unit?"

Minutes later, I was standing in front of Ann.

"He wants the *whole* building."

"The *whole* building?"

"The whole building."

We were both silent, no doubt each dealing with individual struggles. Then Ann asked, "And the Rebbe said to trust him in this?"

"Yes," I replied.

"You actually heard that from the Rebbe?"

"Yes. Those exact words."

"So, what's the question?" Ann asked easily. "We listen to the Rebbe about our health and about the health and futures of our children, why wouldn't we listen to him about this?"

That day, we became $75,000 poorer (our equity in the building), and the first Chabad House in Australia was born.

## FIVE

About ten days later, I was interrupted by my receptionist.

"A Mr. David James is on the phone, will you take his call?"

I remember the shiver that went down my spine, which accompanied many emotions—anger, outrage, and, at the same time, curiosity. When I told her to put him through, I heard, "*Robert*! How *are* you! Long time no see!"

Before I had a chance to answer, he continued, "Are you well? How's the family?"

I have learned to be on guard whenever anyone asks about a family they have never met and whenever someone shakes my hand with two hands.

Ignoring the bustle, I asked with the most deliberately cold voice I could muster, "Why are you ringing me?"

"Can I come and see you?"

"What about?"

"Well, I would rather explain then, but it's trivia."

"I would rather know now," I replied, keeping my voice cold.

His feigned confidence now less certain, he said, "Oh, it's really nothing. We're doing some housekeeping at the insistence of our tiresome accountants. You probably don't remember, but you still have some share or other you needed to put in place when we started. It needs to be transferred to us to tidy things up, so I would like to bring over the paperwork so you can sign it over to us. Can I come now?"

Although caught unawares, I had been sufficiently hurt to remember it all very clearly. Whatever else was going to happen, I wasn't going to allow his original lies to become current bullying.

*chapter 1*

"Of course, I remember. I also remember an arrangement you completely ignored, and I remember that I'm unpaid for the work I did for you."

"Robert, I will explain when I meet you. My board in New Zealand insisted we use brand-name lawyers. I had no say in that. I would, of course, have kept to our arrangement, but my board vetoed it. You know I love you, and I hope you believe me when I say that my hands were tied. The captain isn't always master of the ship. We will give you some work in due course, but I haven't been able to manage it yet. Anyway, that's a whole different story. I'll tell you about it someday over a drink, but I need this paperwork signed today, so can I come over now?"

Smooth as butter.

I don't eat butter.

"No. I want to think about it."

"What?! Think about what? Until when? Come on, Robert, the share is worthless, and it's messing up something major that we're working on."

"I want to think about it. You can ring me tomorrow," I said, hanging up the phone. I realized that I was shaking with anger.

I went home to Ann and poured out my resentment. She understood, of course, but she questioned whether it might make sense to "be nice."

"Why?" I asked.

"Maybe they will come back to you."

I didn't believe that, and I explained why to Ann. I told her that I would charge for the transfer. At first I thought of charging $1,000. But then, on second thought, I figured why not charge the $5,000 I would have earned if he had just paid (the admittedly large) fee like everyone else?

"Five thousand dollars for a signature?" Ann asked with a smile.

"No. It's for the pain and suffering. But," I conceded, "it might be a bit rich."

Ann smiled more broadly.

The next morning I arrived at my office to find David James in my waiting room. He jumped to his feet and dashed over to pump my hand with both of his.

I decided to see him. As I ushered him into my room, I ignored his inquiring how my family was.

Once seated, he pulled a share transfer from a beautiful Florentine leather briefcase while proffering a ridiculously expensive pen.

As he leaned across my desk, I said, "I think I will charge for this, David."

He froze.

"What? Why? It's worthless."

I didn't respond. I looked at him coldly, taking in the silk handkerchief, the glinting gold watch, and the signet ring.

"This is blackmail, Robert!" he exclaimed, which did nothing to improve his position with me.

*chapter 1*

"It's not blackmail. I'm content for you to leave. I have no need to sign anything."

James paused.

"How much do you want for something of no value?"

I remember looking at him and wondering how I had ever thought him charming. Then, from some space I can't identify to this day, I heard myself saying, "$75,000."

"What?" he gasped, and then fell silent. Beginning to perspire slightly, he added, "I won't pay a cent more than $40,000."

So much for his charade. A minute earlier it had been valueless, but now he exposed the lie by counter-offering what should have been a ludicrous amount—$40,000.

"Let me make this simpler for you, David. I have no interest in selling. Truthfully, I also have no interest in helping you. But if I don't have a bank check for $75,000 by four p.m. today, my price will double."

**EPILOGUE**

We were without our contribution to the Chabad House for less than two weeks. Some four hours after he left my office, David James was back in my waiting room with the bank check. I had been fully repaid for our contribution to the Chabad House.

When he came, I didn't go out to see him in the waiting room. My receptionist exchanged the check for the signed transfer agreement. As she brought the money into my room, I heard the Rebbe's words again in my mind, as I still do so many years later, *Trust me in this.*

# It's Only a Flesh Wound

*chapter 2*

### ONE

One day in the early 1980s, I picked up the phone to the familiar voice of Rabbi Feldman.

Rabbi Feldman was many things to me in those days (and still is). Head representative of the Rebbe in Sydney, he ran the Sydney Yeshiva. He was also my pathway to the Rebbe, and he was one of my teachers, but above all, he was a close personal friend.

"I need to retain your services."

New business always being good, I said, "Tell me." I was totally unprepared for what was to follow.

"I have been asked by my friend, a rabbi in The Valley in Los Angeles, to help a young Israeli who is touring Sydney.

Apparently, during his stay he got a job serving hot dogs outside an RSL club."

(For the uninformed reader, these RSL clubs are vast social clubs that provide their members with poker machines, food, and alcohol.)

"He got into an argument with a couple of people who were leaving the RSL, and he ended up stabbing one of them. Unfortunately for him, the person was an off-duty policeman."

This is the sort of legal matter I had no room for. I said, "Sorry, but I don't do criminal law. However, I will recommend someone who does."

"I want you."

I am as vulnerable to compliments as the next man, but that certainly wasn't enough to accept this case.

"Rabbi Feldman, I really don't know much about criminal law. He will be much better off with someone who practices regularly in this jurisdiction and knows the ropes."

"I want you," he repeated.

"Look, I'm flattered, but if you trust my judgement, why not listen to me? You need a criminal lawyer." Then, as an afterthought, I asked, "Has he got any money?"

"Why do you think I want you?"

## TWO

Yigal was waiting for me when I arrived at my office for our 8:30 meeting the next day. We shook hands, and he

*chapter 2*

followed me into my office, sitting immediately and without invitation.

I'm used to taking in new clients fairly quickly, but whatever I had expected, this wasn't it. Sitting before me was a man significantly better looking than any movie star I had ever seen. Aged very early 20s, 6'2" tall, and broad-shouldered, he appeared completely at ease but wild. (What my wife later told me were) dreadlocks fell on a shirt open almost to his navel. On his suntanned chest glinted a large gold Star of David hanging from a large gold chain. His dazzling smile was accentuated by both his suntan and his total relaxation. He exhibited absolutely no insecurity or shyness—qualities usually common to first-time clients, who are anxious about dealing with what—to them—were often novel situations.

"Okay, Yigal, tell me your story."

"No story; I warned the drunken fool again and again. So what could I do? He deserved it. Anyway, it's only a flesh wound. What's all the noise?"

I looked at the copy of the charge sheet my PA had obtained late yesterday.

"Noise? It says here that you are charged with assault and battery."

I looked at Yigal carefully, wondering if he was sane. He merely shrugged his shoulders.

"I had no choice."

"Why? Are you saying it was self-defense?" I decided to explore our first real hope immediately.

## Australian Encounters

"Defense? No. He needed defense. I warned him!" he said with a laugh.

Our chances evaporating, I then asked him to give me a detailed, step-by-step account of what happened. As is often the case, particularly with new clients, this was impossible for him without help; he needed prompts and reminders of what he had already said. Finally, after a half hour of this, I repeated to him the story as I understood it.

He had been working at his hot dog facility when two men, who were obviously well on their way to being totally drunk, lurched towards him from the RSL club. They stopped at the hot dog stand and one of them asked if Yigal had a license. He ignored them. The same man pressed the question while his bloodshot eyes focused on the Star of David. Still Yigal ignored him. Apparently, the other man then joined in, demanding an answer—and respect with that answer. It was then that Yigal smilingly explained, in his broken English, that he had just left the Israeli Army and was fit and strong, while they were two overweight men twice his age. He then generously offered them the advice that they shouldn't start up with him, because to do so would be folly. Appropriately enraged, the first man took a step towards Yigal. Yigal raised his six-inch sausage knife and warned the man that if he took another step he would "open you from your neck to your waist." At this point the second man cautioned Yigal, calling him "Jew-boy." He pointed out that his friend was an off-duty policeman. The policeman then didn't help himself by spluttering that "Hitler knew what to do with your Jew-boy lot." Yigal, bereft of grandparents and extended family, who were all gassed by the Nazis, then took the knife and did exactly as he said he would—he cut the policemen from neck to waist.

### THREE

"Is that a fair summary of what happened," I asked Yigal.

Yigal shrugged his shoulders. "*Ken*" (yes in Hebrew).

I then told him the truth.

"Look, Yigal, your position is very bad. You are clearly guilty of both charges, and there is a very real probability of prison. We can't plead that you are not guilty, because you confess to the truth of what happened, which *is* that you assaulted and battered a policeman. The hate remarks are not enough to warrant your use of the knife, warnings or not."

I paused to see how this was sinking in. Then I said, "I suggest we plead guilty, ask for forgiveness from the policeman, and throw yourself on the mercy of the court by saying how sorry you are. The court may consider the Hitler remark and show some leniency."

Yigal looked at me and then said steadily, "I am not sorry." Then he continued with his sincere assessment of my qualities. "You are not a very good lawyer. Are you Chabad?"

Swallowing my irritation, I confirmed being Chabad.

"Then can you get me a *brachah* (blessing) from the Lubavitcher Rebbe?"

## Australian Encounters

Forcing myself to overlook his charm, this was the best chance we had. I explained that if he wanted a *brachah*, *he* should write in. He was welcome to use my fax machine and be sure to include his Hebrew name and that of his mother. To be clear, at that stage I saw a *brachah* from the Rebbe as our only hope—and even then, I was deeply skeptical that there would be a helpful answer.

Yigal took pen and paper and wrote about three-quarters of a page in Hebrew. To this day I have no idea what he wrote, but I would place a tidy bet that there was some reference to his dissatisfaction with me. We sent the fax, and Yigal began to pack his fringed suede duffle bag with the things he had removed during the conference.

As we walked to the doors of the office, I explained to Yigal that he should wear a suit and tie (still the uniform in the early '80s), and although his hair was no doubt beautiful, he should minimize it in some way.

Yigal looked at me with an expression bordering on contempt, but before the conversation could continue, I heard the noisy sound of the fax machine.

I told him to wait and went back to check. Sure enough, it was one of the Rebbe's secretaries with the answer. The message was astonishing, and I showed the fax to Yigal. *Azkir al hatziyun* ("I will mention it at the grave." It was the Rebbe's practice to read the letters he received at the graveside of the Previous Rebbe. We had learned that this answer was code for the Rebbe giving his blessing.) He looked at the message blankly, so I explained that this was one of the formulas used by the Rebbe when he gave his *brachah*.

"So I have the *brachah*?"

"I believe so."

"You sure?"

"Yes, I'm sure."

"Okay, then, nothing to worry about."

"Well…" I began, but he cut me short.

"The Rebbe says okay, so it will be okay. Are you a believer or not?"

"Of course I am, but what does that mean? I think it means that you should listen to me, and the court will have mercy."

"Are you a rabbi or a lawyer?" Yigal asked irreverently.

"A lawyer," I conceded.

"So, you don't know more than I do."

Definitely difficult to warm to, this self-assured Israeli.

## FOUR

I now had to choose a barrister. Simon Gordon was an old friend with little ego and a generous heart. I explained this was a charity case, as well as a losing proposition, but I really needed him because the client was our biggest problem. I promised that I would give him my next real case in exchange.

Court begins at ten in the morning, and we were first on the list. I had arranged to meet with Yigal and Simon half an hour early to go through the charge sheet and the story one more time. Yigal joined us last, but, to be fair, he wasn't late.

I looked up to see whether a suit would give him a more normal look, but I should have known better. Yigal had made the concession of changing his shirt, but nothing else. The replacement shirt was no less open than the one I had seen earlier. Somehow he looked even more spectacular and wilder in the incongruity of our surroundings. Simon stared at him, and I was conscious of my not warning him about this part.

After the refresher meeting, we made our way to the court and took our seats—Simon at the bar table, me behind him as instructing solicitor, and Yigal to my right. Even after so many years, a courtroom remains intimidating. People sit up a little straighter and are clearly less relaxed. I glanced at Yigal, who was slouched back in his seat, his legs crossed, seemingly as comfortable as if he were about to watch a football match armed with popcorn.

Feldman was going to owe me big time.

The Tipstaff (equivalent to a bailiff) called for all to rise, the judge entered, bowed, and nodded politely to Simon. Astonishingly, the other bar table was empty. Simon lost no time and jumped to his feet.

"Your Honor, the Crown is not present. I move for the case to be dismissed."

"On what grounds, Mr. Gordon?"

*chapter 2*

"The Crown has strict burden of proof, Your Honor, and they are not here. My client is entitled to a dismissal."

"You certainly have a point, Mr. Gordon. Very curious." The judge paused to read the charge sheet. He then continued, "In view of the seriousness of the charges, I will hear another mention [a procedural matter in a court case] and move this case to 10:15 a.m."

Simon sat down, clearly disappointed. Fifteen minutes to wait. My heart was beating, as I am sure was Simon's. The fifteen minutes felt more like fifteen hours. I hardly heard the droning of the mention now ahead of us, my eyes alternating with riveting attention from the door to the clock on the wall.

The mention finished at exactly 10:15, and Simon jumped to his feet.

"Your Honor, I really must insist; my client has his rights. If Your Honor doesn't dismiss, I will reserve our right to appeal."

"There's no need for drama, Mr. Gordon; I am convinced. Let the record show that in the absence of Crown prosecution, the case is dismissed."

Simon and I turned to Yigal in joyful triumph. I'm still not sure he appreciated what had happened. As we were explaining that he was free to go, the clatter of feet could be heard on the stones outside. The court door burst open to a red-faced Crown prosecutor who was clearly unused to the running he had endured to get to the court. A few seconds later the door burst open a second time for the arrival of the luckless victim, who was equally distraught. I no longer remember the exact reasons, but one of them had a car breakdown, and another was on a train that was delayed by a derailment…

As we left the court, if I had expected gratitude, I was wrong. The time spent— for no money and flavored by a good deal of stress—was paid for by Yigal saying, "I will go now. Well, really, you both did nothing. I knew I was okay. I had a *brachah* from the Lubavitcher Rebbe…"

# The Three Problems
*chapter 3*

### ONE

It is important for people whose consciousness of the Lubavitcher Rebbe began after his passing to understand that every person's interaction with the Rebbe was unique. With some the Rebbe was more stern; with others more jovial. Some he rarely answered; others he answered frequently. We never found the key to his actions, other than to universally testify that the Rebbe always wanted more from everyone.

My eldest daughter, Faygele (Nicky), wrote regularly to the Rebbe, and, fascinatingly, she almost always received replies. Mostly, these replies were long in comparison to those received by others in the family. Once—sometime after she finished seminary—she decided to go to New York on her own. We made arrangements for where she would stay, etc., but she was anxious, having heard of the violence taking place at that time in New York and particularly in Crown Heights. She wrote to the Rebbe confiding her fears and received a long answer detailing what to do. The Rebbe itemized which chapters of Psalms to say, how much charity to give before lighting candles on Friday night, to check the *mezuzot* (see Chapter 8), and, finally, a detailed instruction on saying *Tefillat Haderech* (the Traveler's Prayer) repeatedly whenever she felt frightened until the fear would leave. One of her younger sisters, who at that time had normal child night fears, was very impressed, so she sent the Rebbe an equally long letter confiding her fears. She also received a reply, but hers consisted of three words, "*Kriat Shema karagil*" (say the *Shema* before bedtime, as usual).

We noticed that when a person needed an answer, he or she got it, and when they needed a long one, it was long. The inference we supposed was that if the answer was short or non-existent, it was spiritually tailored to the person writing, who certainly did not need more.

## TWO

Nicky married, and she and her husband had their first child in 1993.

When their daughter was about a year or so old, Nicky

*chapter 3*

was overwhelmed with some personal problems relating to certain life choices she had to make.

The reader needs to understand the mindset we all had in differing degrees after the Rebbe's passing. For young people like Nicky, initial shock gave way to a continuing sense of bewilderment. From her perspective, she never knew of a life without the Rebbe. He was the moral, psychological, and spiritual imperative to which everything in her life had always been referenced. One of the foundations of her life, on which she leaned heavily (as we all did), had suddenly been pulled away, leaving her (as with us) staring into the abyss.

### THREE

In 1995, about a year after the Rebbe's passing, we were on holiday in Queensland. We used to rent a house for a month in December (summer in Australia) from absent Chinese investors (who, to the best of my knowledge, never spent a night in the house). The house was huge, on a canal, with a twenty-yard swimming pool and a separate cabana. In those days, Nicky, her husband, and daughter would join us, and we spent many happy summers in this house together with them, our other children, and their friends.

One day I went outside and saw Nicky sitting next to my wife Ann at the edge of the pool. They were deep in conversation, and Ann signaled to me not to disturb them. It was obvious that poor Nicky had been crying bitterly, because her face was swollen and her eyes were red. I scurried away, confident that if my help was needed, either of them would tell me in due course.

Soon enough, I was informed that Nicky had three separate and unrelated problems, any one of which would be overwhelming for someone suffering from the black dog of depression. All three together were crippling, and she had been crying, unable to find any direction.

It is important to note that in that early time after the Rebbe's passing, rank and file Chabad members were still confused about how to communicate with the Rebbe. Of course, we knew from *Tanya* (and this was suddenly publicized frequently) that the soul of a righteous person after his passing was more available to those connected to him than when he was alive. The reason for this is that the soul is no longer bound by the restrictions of the body, and its power is therefore greater. But how to communicate? At that time it was difficult to get a consensus.

One method, then in its infancy, was to write a letter and place it in a volume of the *Igrot Kodesh*.

In the interest of truth, the reader needs to understand an important caveat to what is to follow. Although the Rebbe said that if a person sought connection to the Previous Rebbe after his passing, the Previous Rebbe "would find a way," any such way is individual and is in no way enshrined by our tradition. To quote a method as having its own pedigree is therefore false. It would be equally false, however, not to recognize that pathways exist for individuals, albeit

*chapter 3*

dependent on too many variables to be hallowed into general acceptance.

At that time, the *Igrot Kodesh* consisted of twenty-five volumes of the Rebbe's letters, written to people over the years of his leadership. The letters covered the Rebbe's advice to his followers on every conceivable subject, ranging from the physical to the spiritual. Some people had the idea that if a person placed his request in one of these volumes (together some 10,000 pages) and there was a correlation of subject matter on the relevant page, the Rebbe was answering the writer. Again it is important to point out that this method, like every other, is at best individual and certainly not sanctioned by any of our Rebbes. Equally, what is to follow really happened, and I feel I would be dishonest without telling it.

Ann pointed out to Nicky that she needed advice. The Rebbe's letters contained advice for many of life's challenges. Why not look there?

The suggestion brought Nicky to fresh tears. How could the Rebbe have left her? How could the Rebbe have left us? And which of her three problems should she ask about? Not having her accustomed access to the Rebbe just intensified her sadness.

Ann was firm but gentle. Either Nicky believed in what it says in *Tanya* or she didn't. If she did, why would three questions be more difficult than one? Why not seek advice about whatever she needed and leave it to the Rebbe to find a way to answer her?

## FOUR

Nicky eventually came around to the idea of writing a letter to the Rebbe. It took some time while she discussed it with her husband and prepared herself, but within a couple of days she produced folded paper and began to look for a volume of the *Igrot Kodesh*.

Fortunately, the Chabad rabbi near where we were staying had a set, so my son-in-law drove Nicky to his house.

There she chose a volume at random, inserted her letter, and listened while her husband read and translated the letters on the double page. By Divine Providence, the first letter contained advice that caused Nicky to almost faint.

The letter her husband read was addressed to a woman, not a man. It opened by expressing surprise that she had taken so long to write, particularly considering the past frequency of correspondence. The letter then proceeded to quote the same three questions and answer them one by one!

Not only that, but the answers were in the specific order that Nicky had written the questions!

## FIVE

There is nothing more to say about this story. The resultant effect on our entire family was predictable and mammoth. Who could doubt the window into seeing this marvel and all that it implies?

# Would You Do It for Me?
*chapter 4*

**ONE**

My father passed away in 1975 at the age of sixty-five. The cause of death was cancer, which had gone undetected almost until the end. Earlier diagnosis would not have helped much in any case, because in those days most forms of cancer were a death sentence.

When he passed away, Ann and I were already on our journey to becoming practicing Jews. Although my father did not approve, this became relevant for my mother, as you will see.

If my father was young to die, my mother was even younger to be widowed. Although we never knew my mother's age (kept obsessively secret by her), we placed her about ten years younger than my father.

After his passing, I arranged the sale of their house, paid off the remaining mortgage, and with the proceeds I bought my mother an unencumbered apartment some five hundred yards away from our home. Although my in-laws were wonderful to her, taking her on all their many outings, and although we were careful to provide her with care and plentiful access to the grandchildren, she became increasingly lonely.

After being a widow for eight years, I decided to try to get her to remarry. During those eight years, as Ann and I became more observant—and probably as a means to connect with us—my mother began to renew the observances she remembered from her parents' home in her native Poland. They had been swept away many years earlier by my father's anger at G-d for the Holocaust. She started by making her kitchen kosher so we and the children could eat there, and from there she progressed to being—as much as possible for her—fully observant.

## TWO

There was a man in our synagogue named Max Weidman, who had consulted me about his divorce. Lawyers see people under stress, and I was impressed to see that despite the temptations of that pressure, he exhibited decency and fundamental integrity. He never talked his wife down, simply accepting that they could no longer live together. I later

*chapter 4*

found out that he had plenty to complain about, but he kept silent, which earned my respect.

I resolved to introduce him to my mother, and with hesitant permission from both of them, I did so.

Max was religiously observant but conflicted. The war had taken its toll (he had witnessed his just-teenaged sister shot in front of him by a smiling Nazi), but unlike my father, he continued keeping the *mitzvot*. My mother overcame her natural wariness at their unequal financial position (he had abdicated everything to his wife in the divorce) and tuned in to his positives.

They were married a short time later in a religious ceremony in the Sydney Yeshiva—a place in which I would never have dreamed to see my mother until recently. The wedding brought significant ambivalent emotions for me—happiness for my mother's new chance in life versus an only child with no relatives watching his mother marry another man. Generally, however, everyone in the family approved. Max moved into my mother's apartment, and they began their new observant life together.

### THREE

In those days, the Shabbat family dynamic was that everyone came to us for the Friday night meal. My in-laws and Ann's sister did not keep our standard of kosher, and it was easier to keep one standard. We would also have other guests. We have a large dining room, and our table seats fourteen without an extension. My in-laws and sister-in-law seldom joined us for the Shabbat day meal, but the guest component was often larger.

A few years into their marriage, Max was struck with the agony of a kidney stone and was basically immobilized for about a week. For the happily uninitiated, kidney stones are of various sizes, spherical, and with a jagged outside edge. After formation, they move down the urinary tract. As they move, they roll, and their jagged edge tears the flesh, resulting in tortuous pain.

A new technology had become available to those blighted by this terribly painful condition, which involved a laser beam breaking up the stone.

My mother and Max were uncharacteristically absent that Friday night. We sent one of the children to check on them and found that Max was again in great pain. On Shabbat day, however, we were relieved to find them already at our house when we returned from *shul*. We joined up at the table, and I made *Kiddush* as usual.

Seating at our table in those days followed an unplanned but repetitive dynamic—Max sat on my left, and my mother sat next to him. When they were there, my father-in-law was on my right with my mother-in-law next to him. The remaining seating devolved in some sort of perceived importance of people, with the children taking up those seats left over, or, on a busy Shabbat, those at the extension of the table.

*chapter 4*

This Shabbat was quiet; it was just us and our four children, plus my mother and Max. On such days, the children availed themselves of the "important" seats, and this Shabbat there was enough room for everyone without fighting. My son, Akiva, then eight or nine years old, was sitting about halfway down the table diagonally opposite Max under the framed photograph of the Rebbe, which hung in a commanding place in our dining room.

**FOUR**

A short time into the meal, my mother expressed her worry that Max was to be operated on the following Tuesday. The operation was the aforementioned laser procedure. The usual conversation followed—where, when, who was doing it, etc. Max, pale and drawn from the week's ordeal, made the point that he couldn't wait for the procedure. Apparently, Max needed to go in on Monday, with the procedure set for Tuesday morning.

It was then that Akiva asked the question.

Before I continue, some background is necessary. This was the late 1980s. The Rebbe was well, and the idea that we would one day be without his physical presence was unthinkable. Our children lived the cloistered lives of Chabad children, busy with *yeshivah*, after-school *cheder* (for additional learning), *mesibot Shabbat* (children's gatherings) on Shabbat afternoon, and *cheder* again on Sunday. The towering shadow of the Rebbe enthused children to focus their ambition on being like him. Children respected their parents, and, by and large, with limited access to TV and no computers yet, they escaped the insane environment of the outside world.

Therefore, when Akiva asked the question, it was that of a little boy mouthing something totally standard in his life without much thought; it was almost automatic.

"Have you written in to the Rebbe yet?"

Max turned to Akiva, and, showing his developed fondness for him, spoke kindly and gently.

"I don't write in, Akiva."

This simply didn't compute, and Akiva asked, "What do you mean?"

"Well, the way I grew up, we had no tradition of Rebbes. Our perspective is that all Jews have direct access to G-d, and there is no need or value to an intermediary."

Akiva's face was blank. Max could have been talking in Chinese. To a child who from birth lived in a family where the Rebbe was the intellectual, psychological, and moral standard, Max's words simply had no meaning.

"Dad, what does he mean?"

I had to be careful. This was my mother's husband. On the other hand, my son's education was suddenly vulnerable. Instead of answering Akiva, I remember addressing Max.

"Maybe you can explain why in our daily prayers we say that the Children of Israel *believed in G-d and in Moses, his servant*".

*chapter 4*

Max ignored the question, and, addressing Akiva, simply said, "Anyway, son, I don't write to any Rebbe."

"But this is the *Rebbe*," Akiva said, clearly still not understanding.

Akiva's eyes became glassy.

"And you're going to have *an operation*."

"Yes."

"Without trying to get a *brachah*?!"

"Yes."

There was silence at the table. Akiva was struggling and finally melted into tears.

"Well, Max, *would you do it for me?*"

It was now time for Max's eyes to become glassy. He paused and then, almost whispering, he said, "Yes. For *you*, I will."

Max was true to his word. After Shabbat, he wrote a letter and brought it to me so I could fax it to the Rebbe's office. The letter was in Yiddish, and I sent it without reading it, of course (not that I could in any case). I warned Max, new to this dynamic, that he might not receive a reply. The Rebbe received two sacks of mail a day and often there were no answers. Late on Sunday night, however, we received a reply. Akiva, overjoyed, grabbed the phone to be the first to tell Max that he had a reply.

The reply said three things: *azkir al hatziyun* ("I will mention it at the grave [of the Previous Rebbe]," which, as explained in a previous chapter was understood as code for

35

"you have the blessing"); secondly, and unusually in view of the first line, *refuah shleimah b'karov*, which means "a complete recovery soon"; and, finally, *bedikat hamezuzot*, which is an instruction to check the *mezuzot* to see if they remain kosher.

Akiva didn't care. Life was progressing according to his reality. The Rebbe had replied and given his *brachah*, so all would be well.

## FIVE

In the introduction I pledged pristine truth, so my description of the medical part of this story is deliberately general. However, certain broad brush strokes are available. The procedure was fixed for Tuesday. Max was to be admitted Monday afternoon. Apparently, some sort of X-ray had to be taken on Monday night to check the size and whereabouts of the stone. The result showed the stone as about half the size of a pea—which for kidney stones is monstrous. On Tuesday morning another such X-ray was mandated to ensure that the stone hadn't moved.

Max was wheeled to the operating theater to lie helplessly in a cubicle waiting his turn.

Suddenly, two doctors and one nurse appeared in his cubicle.

The first doctor told Max that he could not explain it, but he was certain there was no mistake: the X-ray showed that there was no kidney stone! It had simply vanished! The

*chapter 4*

doctor explained it was impossible, because it had been there the previous night, and Max couldn't have possibly passed it. If he had, the whole hospital would have heard the screams, and perhaps the surrounding suburb, as well. Nevertheless, there was no stone, and, therefore, there was to be no procedure.

My mother kept the discharge sheet. Under the heading "Discharge," the hospital had written the words "Rabbinic Miracle."

My mother and Max were, of course, absolutely bewildered. Max thanked Akiva for prompting the *brachah* and understandably began to move closer to Chabad.

They subsequently went to New York to see the Rebbe. Later, and at his request, I began to learn the Rebbe's teachings with Max before *davening* (praying).

I can still see my little boy's earnest face and hear his words, "Well, Max, *would you do it for me?*"

# Nothing

## *chapter 5*

In about 2005, my mother-in-law began to experience pain in her upper body. I say upper body because she wasn't sure where the pain was coming from. At varying times it seemed to be coming from her throat, her chest, or more specifically from her breast. One thing was certain: the pain was slowly but steadily increasing.

Of course, she went to the doctor. Unable to confidently determine the cause, the doctor referred her to a specialist, who predictably ordered a battery of tests.

The tests showed a growth, but the cause of the growth was unclear. The specialist referred her to another specialist.

The second specialist was an expert on breast cancer and confided to my mother-in-law that she herself was living with breast cancer, and in her case it was manageable. However, my mother-in-law's growth worried her, because she suspected that it wasn't manageable, and she therefore recommended an exploratory operation.

My mother-in-law balked at this, because both specialists were still unsure of a diagnosis. However, the second one told her that if her suspicions were correct, my mother-in-law would only have a few months to live. Her only chance was an investigative procedure to determine the degree of malignancy consistent with the lump's rapid growth. If malignant, it could be cut out on the spot. Furthermore, the doctor ruled that it was most urgent and nominated a surgeon.

The family was shocked. The situation had developed quickly, and no one was mentally ready to adjust from seeing my mother-in-law being fully healthy with just a bit of pain to the prospect of looming death.

A date was set for the operation.

Ann reserves some quiet time for prayer after lighting the candles on Friday night. It's not uncommon for her to stand at the candles for ten minutes or so, eyes closed and obviously deeply focused. I know that it's her time for both thanking G-d for our blessings and asking for the welfare of members of our family. Her concentration is obvious, and the children have learned—if they're in the house—to give her space during that time.

The Friday after the date was set for the operation was a night of copious rain, and I stayed home from *shul*. I was

*chapter 5*

surprised to notice that Ann was at the candles for at least double her usual time, and when she finished her eyes were red. I understood immediately that she was praying for her mother.

On Sunday, my wife asked her sister to visit so they could write to the Rebbe together by placing the letter in a volume of *Igrot Kodesh* (see Chapter 3).

Inevitably, I heard what they had written, and I was privately a bit displeased. The women had spelled out the problem and the need for the operation, and, in my wife's words, they asked the Rebbe for a *brachah* "that it was nothing."

Ann picked up on my discontent and questioned me. I explained that I didn't understand how they could ask for something impossible. They could ask that the tumor be benign and for a successful excision, but what was the point of asking for something that was plainly impossible?! What could that possibly achieve?

The sisters huddled and discussed the position while I attended to something else. Then, calling me to show them which were the volumes of the *Igrot Kodesh*, my wife informed me that their letter remained unchanged. They wanted a *brachah* that it was nothing.

They inserted the letter, and I read the two pages for them. Nothing relevant seemed apparent other than a general blessing for an unrelated subject in one of the letters.

The operation took place that week.

A biopsy was taken and the offending material was removed and sent for analysis. The analysis took some time and the result uncertain. It was then sent overseas for further analysis.

Meanwhile, of course, the family lived with growing tension.

After what seemed like a never-ending delay, my mother-in-law was notified of the result.

It was a piece of carrot!

A piece of carrot had somehow been waylaid (I don't have the medical knowledge to describe this), and cells had accumulated around it, forming the lump visible on the image.

My wife was crying when she repeated the specialist's words: "We are delighted to report that it was nothing."

# Brian Rimband QC

*chapter 6*

**ONE**

The world was a very different place when I graduated from law school in 1966.

There was no such notion as political correctness, snobbery was alive and well, and inventions like Kleenex did not exist. Before the pop music industry suddenly exploded like a mushroom-shaped cloud, behavior was very regimented. Dress codes were strict, manners an absolute necessity, and conformity not only basic but essential.

The women's movement was still in its infancy. In my class of about two hundred graduates, there were three women, who carefully avoided the bad behavior of their male classmates—who drank and caroused their way through law school.

In those days, only about two percent of the population had been to university. Those who had were guaranteed disproportionate wealth and unquestioned authority when mixing with the "lower echelons" of "ordinary" people.

The '60s and '70s took a strong broom to all that, sweeping away bastions of conservative institutionalized life. Woodstock began as a revolution but remained an irrepressibly developing new norm.

An exception to this new process was my friend from law school, Brian Rimband. We were good friends from our undergraduate studies for arts degrees through law school, and we frequently sat next to each other during lectures. Rimband was a flagship of the time's social mores. He was from a "good home," went to a "good school," and was extremely capable academically. He was also proudly cultured, quoting the Jacobean poets from our earlier days, and he was a frequent attendee of all the good concerts that took place in the then-culturally starved Sydney. He was tall, slim, and good looking in a WASPish sort of way. Of course, his hair was short (until the Beatles, long hair was unthinkable), and his clothing—the uniform of suit and tie—were neat and clean. In those days, I knew absolutely nothing of Judaism, and having spent all my school life in a "very good school," I spoke "Rimbandese" as a primary language and second nature.

*chapter 6*

After law school, we went our separate ways. I opened a law practice, and Brian went to the Bar to practice as a barrister. We were both successful, and every few years I used to brief him [the process of a solicitor providing a barrister with a case in the British justice system after which the Australian system is modeled] if I had a suitable case. These became fewer as Brian quickly began to specialize in the rarefied jurisdiction of the equity courts, where giant corporations were the only ones that could afford passage.

My practice became more and more property oriented, and eventually we reached the point where our paths rarely crossed.

Brian took silk (became Queen's Counsel), grew to be very well known, and, incidentally (without ever mentioning anything so crass, of course), made a good deal of money.

## TWO

The person who was probably my best property client in the early to mid-'80s was a likeable and slightly mischievous charmer in his late fifties named Bob Driver. Bob was a property developer and very lucky. He bought property in dangerous transactions, and always came out on the other side with huge profits. He didn't work very hard, played a lot of golf very well, and bridge very badly. He was a great salesman of himself and what he did, always boasting to his ever-present listeners that life was easy—all you had to do was make the right choices. Confusingly for others, he seemed to have endless money.

One day, he arrived at my office uncharacteristically red-faced and distraught. Outraged, and with his voiced raised, he said, "You will never believe what's happened!"

"What?"

"I've been charged with a criminal offense!"

He might have been a mover and shaker, but, at least until now, Bob was no criminal.

"What's the charge?"

"Bribery!"

"*Bribery*?! Who?"

"This peanut Johnson at the Snowy Mountains Authority."

The story unfolded. Driver was developing a building in the snow country that he had bought for a song, risking that he would receive permission from the Snowy Mountains Authority to convert it into apartments. Consent would allow him to configure it into ten apartments, which would net him a small fortune. However, no consent was forthcoming for over a year. Finally, in exasperation, Driver flew down to see the clerk in charge, a man named Johnson, and gave him two hundred dollars. Although a reasonable sum in the mid-'80s, it obviously wasn't enough, because unbeknownst to Driver, Johnson promptly reported him. Shortly thereafter he was charged and released on bail.

Driver was furious.

*chapter 6*

"*Bail.*" he spat. "What have I got to do with *bail*?! *Charged*. What have I got to do with *charged*?"

I read the charge sheet, and sure enough Bob was charged with bribing an officer of Her Majesty's authority. The charge sheet conveniently and obligingly pointed out that the maximum sentence for this offense was five years in prison.

Truthfully, I was shocked. But typically for him, Driver moved straight to action.

"Listen carefully, Robert. I want the best lawyer in the country. Get me the best barrister; I don't care what it costs." His eyes narrowed and he added, "And let's be clear: Your practice won't be worth two cents if anything goes wrong."

Sensing his genuine anguish, I ignored the temptation to take offense, and I asked him to leave it with me.

This was a problem, indeed. I am not a criminal lawyer, and I don't know my way around the nasty dungeons of the criminal world. On the other hand, Driver was my best client, probably accounting for twenty-five percent of our gross fees. Therefore, apart from wanting to look after him, success was vital to me. Separately, referring him elsewhere meant risking losing my best client.

### THREE

I decided to ring Brian Rimband.

It wasn't an immediate success. Brian, almost amused at the suggestion, patiently explained that his life was in the equity courts. "Criminal court, dear boy," as he put it, was for a lower level of humanity. Why not wait until I had a decent case involving real law, "and then, dear boy," he would accommodate our friendship and take a case I referred.

However, the matter was too important for me to be daunted. I passionately explained how critical it was for me personally, reminded him that twenty years earlier I had lent him my notes, which got him through an exam at law school, and that I was calling in that favor. Finally, I told him clearly that I was begging. His last attempt to wrench free of me was to tell me that he charged $10,000 per day (an unheard-of sum in ordinary courts).

I went back to Driver, explained my choice, and the problem of the money.

"I'll pay it if you assure me he is the best."

"He's the best I know."

"Okay. Let's go and win."

## FOUR

The matter was heard in Kogarah Court, a court of Petty Sessions. The place was so awful that it almost defies description. The overall sense of the place was of entering a large public toilet. People I thankfully usually had nothing to do with were lounging around awaiting their turn to be heard. Petty thieves, drug dealers, wife beaters, and those accused of minor assault and battery charges were the background music for the day. The magistrate (the place didn't

*chapter 6*

warrant a judge) was someone Brian and I knew from law school twenty years earlier. The poor fellow looked like Sad Sack, a tired and strained cartoon character from my youthful years. When he saw Rimband enter his courtroom, he almost stood up in respectful shock at the incongruity of his presence there.

Practically apologizing, the magistrate told Brian that we were about a third of the way down the list and wouldn't be reached before 11:30. He regretted the strain on Brian's time, but the list was fixed.

Brian smoothly assured him that he understood completely and would take a walk with his instructing solicitor. The hapless client paying him $10,000 for the day did not get a mention, nor, indeed, even a look. Brian took my arm, pointedly telling Driver that he wanted to discuss the case without him. We left the court, leaving an annoyed Driver to wait.

### FIVE

In Chapter 12, I explain the whole background to the Machne Israel Development Fund. In short, membership in the organization meant the ability to have private audiences with the Lubavitcher Rebbe.

In the twenty years since law school, I had become almost unrecognizable to Brian. I had begun, and advanced considerably on, a journey to become a fully-observant Jew. I now wore a yarmulke and beard. Torah had become the central focus of my life. I drank thirstily from its wisdom whenever possible, given the strictures of family and business. My wife had accompanied me on this adventure, and our children knew no other life. By the time we stepped out of Kogarah Court, Rimband and I only had memories in common.

My wife and I had just returned from New York, where we had had a private audience with the Rebbe. Many people from around the world had come for this privilege, and before the Rebbe met people individually, he would deliver a *sichah* (a talk) to everyone as a group. On this occasion, the Rebbe said many things during the *sichah*, but I will summarize part of it. The Rebbe reminded us that G-d creates the universe and all that is in it at every moment. This entails His *control* over everything He is bringing into existence. This Divine Providence therefore extends also to the time in which we live and the people we meet. We suppose that those we meet are random, but a moment's thought shows how impossible this is. It follows that everyone we businessmen meet, we meet *purposefully*. It is our task to use any such interaction to do good and help anyone G-d brings our way to grow. When returning home, we should be careful with the truth, answer all questions honestly and fully, and seek to join any such person to ourselves as moral imperatives in our respective environments.

## SIX

It was therefore unnerving when no sooner had we started walking that Brian said, "I understand you just returned from the States. Holiday?"

I nearly simply confirmed his assumption. What would Brian want to know of Jews, Torah, and the Rebbe? But the words of the Rebbe in that *sichah* glowed in my mind like a neon sign, and I heard myself answering, eyes almost closed in the anxiety of being totally not understood, "No. I went to see my Rebbe."

The earth didn't open up. We were still walking. My White Anglo-Saxon Protestant friend from yesteryear was simply quiet. After a pause, Brian asked, "What is a Rebbe?"

This was the moment of truth. What was I to do? I'm not an evangelist. My story and his had become so different that we had few possible points of contact outside of our profession. I decided I would answer any question truthfully but volunteer nothing.

I needn't have been concerned. There was no time for volunteering anything. Brian was relentless. He wanted to know what a Rebbe is, what Torah is, why we Jews keep commandments, what gives a Rebbe power to give blessings, how do these blessings work, what is the status of miracles, can a real Rebbe perform them? I answered everything truthfully and as fully as I could. He wanted to know what made me change direction in life, observing that the change was substantial. I tried, as frankly as possible, to explain the sense of purpose, fulfillment, and happiness I had found.

By the time we returned to court, both Brian and I shared a paradox. On the one hand, our distance in our way of life had been articulated. On the other hand, we were somehow closer, having shared something we both felt was more important than the usual small talk. Furthermore, I also remembered marveling at how completely Brian had absorbed everything.

## SEVEN

We were called and Brian disposed of the case in about twenty minutes. Driver was, of course, ecstatic, immediately forgiving his abandonment while Brian steered me to walk with him an hour and a half earlier.

> [By the way, if you're wondering how he won, I will summarize. Johnson was called to the stand, and after telling his bribery story to the prosecutor, he was cross-examined by Rimband. That cross was nothing short of masterful. Slowly and kindly, Brian dealt with many formalities; married, children, normal functional life, keen gardener. The longer the exchange, the more visibly Johnson began to relax. Rimband observed how tidy Johnson seemed, which was met with a gush of gratitude that this had been noticed. Johnson was obviously proud of this private discipline. Then, as smoothly as silk, Brian wondered

whether Johnson was tidy enough to know what time Driver gave him the money. Leaning on the fact that this great barrister had noticed his discipline, Johnson said of course. He was allowed to prove this without interruption. He had specifically looked at the clock because he remembered he was hungry.

"And what time was it when you looked?"

"It was 1:10 p.m."

"Are you sure?" purred Rimband.

"Of course I'm sure," replied Johnson, now comfortable that his exactitude had been well developed between this respectful stranger and himself.

Brian then referred him to the charge sheet and asked if he could see the approval stamp of the Authority. Did he see the time on the stamp? Would he please read it for the court?

"12:53 p.m."

"Really? 12:53 p.m.? Thank you, Mr. Johnson, I have no further questions."

The witness was dismissed.

Brian put it to the magistrate that since the approval

> was *before* the handing over of the money, the money had the status of a thank-you *present*, not a bribe to induce consent. The magistrate took no further time disposing of the matter.]

We all shook hands amidst the smiles of success and said our goodbyes, with Driver promising to add an expensive bottle of single-malt whiskey to Rimband's fee.

## EIGHT

I arrived back at the office to find a message to ring Rimband.

"Does your holy man in New York give his 'brokers' (his attempt at pronouncing *brachot*) to gentiles? More specifically, would he give one to me and my wife?"

I then listened in surprise and considerable empathy while Brian proceeded to pour his heart out in his perfect, clipped, educated accent.

Brian filled in the twenty years. He had married a stage actress named Violet, and they had three sons. Blessed with money, fame, and happiness, their only tension was Brian's stuffy and reactionary demeanor scratching against Violet's outgoing Bohemian one. Still, they managed to find their compromises, and really all was well.

All three boys were at boarding school (the one outside Melbourne that had been attended by Prince Charles).

## chapter 6

However, the middle one was involved in some sort of accident while at camp and had died.

Brian and Violet's lives changed instantly. They grieved terribly.

Brian had not gone to his chambers (law office) for months, and Violet wouldn't take calls from her theater friends.

In due course they decided to try to heal their wounds by having another child.

"And that's why I'm ringing you, dear boy."

"I don't understand."

Patiently, Brian continued with his story without it occurring to him that I might have anything else on my plate.

They had learned that Violet was expecting a girl.

"That's wonderful, Brian."

The story was uncharacteristically personal, and I felt the closeness of his decision to include me in the knowledge, but I still had no idea where this was going.

"Well, it's not so wonderful. Slowly but increasingly, Violet became depressed, and she is now bedridden. She is terrified that because she is over forty, the baby may be born deformed. She is so desperately depressed that I am seriously concerned that she may commit suicide."

"I see."

"So, dear boy, can I write to the Rebbe?"

This was a novel question for me. On the one hand, neither Brian nor Violet were Jewish, but on the other hand, I thought, so what?

I asked for time and rang my friend, Rabbi Feldman, the Rebbe's head representative in Sydney. His answer was short, and I could feel him smiling through the phone.

"I don't understand. Are you asking if the Rebbe needs you to be his censor?!"

Duly humbled, I went back to Brian with the address.

However, I wanted to warn him that he might not receive a reply. We, who had a relationship with the Rebbe, sadly accepted that of the two sacks of mail the Rebbe received every day, only some were answered. People broke their heads trying to find a pattern to the replies, but to no avail. Important and good people wrote for years without answer, and the most improbable people received long and meticulous instructions.

"Dear boy, *of course* he will answer me." Not being replied to was unthinkable for B. Rimband QC.

"Indeed, to be certain, I will write on my letterhead."

I sighed inwardly and wished him luck after commiserating on his sad position.

## NINE

About ten days later, my direct line rang. It was Brian.

"Dear boy, I just thought I would let you know that I got the broker."

"*Really*? The Rebbe replied?"

*chapter 6*

"*Of course* he did, my dear chap. I was never in doubt. But, more importantly, he gave us the broker."

I was so happy for him. My head was spinning, remembering the *sichah* and the walk in Kogarah; I marveled at the Rebbe's reach.

I asked, if it wasn't too personal, if Brian could tell me the reply.

"Of course, dear boy. The Rebbe blessed Violet and the pregnancy, and he said that the baby would be born at the proper time. Furthermore, he told Violet to trust in the Almighty and not worry because worry cannot achieve anything positive, and also she and the baby would be fine.

"He then added that I should affix a charity box to somewhere in the house and be careful to deposit a coin or two regularly."

"Wow."

I wondered if Brian knew what he had; whether he understood the strength of the guarantees. But he had an instruction, and I felt bound to explain that we knew that when the Rebbe gave a *brachah* and an instruction, the *brachah* was contingent on the instruction. I tried to tell him tactfully.

Silence. Then, "Robert, the first thing I did when I received the letter was to go out and buy the biggest charity box I could find. I had it nailed to the bannister in our entrance hall, where I will use it every day of my life."

I was so happy. Then I made a bad mistake.

"And how is Violet?"

This silence dwarfed the last. Eventually Brian almost whispered, "How can *you* ask me that?"

After a further pause, he went on to tell me that she jumped out of bed the day he received the letter and is now totally unrecognizable. She is happy, optimistic, and decorating a room for the new nursery.

"But how, dear boy, can *you* ask me how she is?!"

Much time has passed—almost another thirty years.

I'm sure the reader has learned from my mistake and doesn't need to ask about Violet's beautiful married daughter…

# What's in a Name?

*chapter 7*

**ONE**

It was about 1975. I had met Rabbi Feldman and others at the Sydney Yeshiva about six months before this incident. At that time, my Jewish knowledge was bordering on zero. To give the reader a measure, I had never heard of Sukkot, or indeed anything other than Rosh Hashanah and Yom Kippur. Even the latter were just names to me, having no idea of what was supposed to happen on those days.

In my new-found relationship with Rabbi Feldman, there were two powerful currents. He was in Sydney to teach Jews how to be Jews. At the same time, he was always desperately short of money.

I had begun my journey towards observance and found

it interesting and even intoxicating. But at the time of this incident, I knew almost nothing.

I had opened my practice as a lawyer some six years earlier. Many of my clients were referred to me by my father-in-law.

King Hu Loo was one of them.

King was a Chinese business associate of my father-in-law's. He lived in Hong Kong, and both he and my father-in-law were well-placed to help each other, because they were both in the fashion industry.

On one of his many trips to Sydney, he came to see me with the following proposition. He had a brief to buy a building for the Philippine government that would be used as their consulate in Sydney, and he wanted me to find a suitable building that would fit the description he would give me. We would buy the building and flip it to the Philippine government, which would net a handsome profit. When I raised the need for proper disclosure, he assured me that he would never make a secret commission, and, of course, our profit would be disclosed.

I went to work and in time found a suitable building. Contracts were drawn up, and King flew to Sydney to sign. I added a clause to the contract setting out how much we paid, the resale price, our exact profit, and an acknowledgement that the Philippine government was aware of this profit. When he saw the clause, King exploded and asked if I was

*chapter 7*

mad. Of course he had made full disclosure to his *friend*, but this was like a red flag to a bull.

We argued for some time; I explained to King that this could be a criminal offense and that without the clause I didn't want anything to do with being a partner in the transaction. King remained adamant. I withdrew from the matter, but I explained to King that I was doing so on condition that my share be paid to charity. I told him truthfully that I didn't think he should benefit from my withdrawal, and, to be fair to him, he agreed without argument. Since I was acting as the solicitor on the transaction, he signed an authority for me to deduct the amount that I was to give to a charity of my choice in his name. (The attorney/client relationship entitles a client to have his lawyer believe him unless he has actual proof to the contrary. Since I didn't have proof, I continued to act as his solicitor, but my discomfort forced me to withdraw from being a principal in the transaction.)

I then had the pleasure of ringing Rabbi Feldman with the news that King Hu Loo, a Chinese gentile who had probably met less than a dozen Jews in his life, was about to donate a serious amount of money to the Sydney Yeshiva.

## TWO

My father was in the hospital, dying from a yet-undiagnosed cancer. During one of my daily visits, he informed me that he disapproved of my venturing into religion, explaining that he had tried to spare me "all of that" because he was unforgivingly angry with G-d for allowing the Holocaust. However, since I could not be dissuaded, it was only right that I should know a few things. First, our family name had originally been Horowitz; second, I was a Levite (I had no idea what that meant); and third, the name "Kremnitzer" came from my direct ancestor, who was the Rebbe in a town in Poland (now Ukraine) called Kremnitz. When my parents escaped Poland, the only country that would grant them a visa was India, where my father dropped the "t" from our name as a concession to help the locals pronounce the name.

## THREE

Rabbi Feldman was naturally delighted with what was a large and unexpected windfall, and he felt it necessary to have a little ceremony to express the Yeshiva's gratitude to King Hu Loo. I still have a picture in my mind of the bewildered Chinese businessman sucking on a large (habitual) cigar, surrounded by Jews, who, to him, looked like they were from another planet.

## FOUR

After the ceremony, Rabbi Feldman asked me to join him in his office together with the teacher with whom I had started lessons, Rabbi Kantor.

There, Rabbi Feldman asked me something I found completely bewildering. He wanted me to write to the Lubavitcher Rebbe. I had never heard of him. Why should I

*chapter 7*

write to someone I didn't know? Rabbi Feldman was evasive. What should I write about? Rabbi Feldman replied that he didn't want to structure the letter in any way. But surely if he was asking me, there must be some reason, and perhaps I could include that reason in my letter. Rabbi Feldman just repeated that it was his request and it was up to me. I told him I would dictate something to my secretary the next day, but they both disabused me of this plan, explaining that the letter had to be handwritten on an unlined piece of paper (standard protocols when writing to the Rebbe).

I left his office mystified.

A day or two later I sat down to write. But I still didn't know what to write.

To this day, my cheeks burn in embarrassment whenever I think of that letter.

I wrote something to the effect that I was sending greeting to a Rebbe, and I knew what that was, because I myself was a bit of a Rebbe. I knew that from my father's disclosure, which I described, and I was sure that the guys in Kremnitz must have known the guys in Lubavitch. Since he and I had Rebbe-ness in common, I wished him well and passed on what I was sure would be regards from Rabbi Feldman and Rabbi Kantor. Furthermore, if he ever needed advice or even a chat, I was happy to provide it free of charge.

Can you imagine how I feel whenever I torture myself remembering that letter?

## Australian Encounters

The reader may not be surprised to learn that I didn't receive an answer…

### FIVE

Nine years passed. My wife and I found our way to observant Judaism. Although I was still terribly embarrassed by my first letter, I began to write to the Rebbe as I learned more about about him and became influenced by him. I never received a reply.

When our eldest daughter reached the age of high school, we decided to try to create one since Chabad didn't have one yet. Every Wednesday night, we would go to the homes of girls who didn't attend Jewish schools and try to sell our new jewel of a school to their parents (and to them, as well). When we had filled our quota, I wrote to the Rebbe to report and ask for a *brachah* for our new school.

I received my first-ever reply promptly by airmail. The letter contained a blessing, but both the envelope and the letter inside were curiously addressed. My name was spelled "Kremnich," and the "n" in both the letter and the envelope seems to have been altered by the Rebbe in ink. This unusual spelling seems to reflect its origins, to which I had referred in my embarrassing letter.

I still have the letter and envelope. I remain in wonder at the fact that the Rebbe remembered, nine years later, receiving such a letter from an ignorant Jew on the other side of the world, about nothing! And, incredibly, he found a way of

*chapter 7*

singling out that Jew's existence, by acknowledgment, while giving his blessing.

# Dr. Frank and the Miracle That Didn't Happen

*chapter 8*

**ONE**

In 1986, I began to give a *shiur* (class) in my home on Tuesday nights at 8:30 p.m. Thirty-six years later, it is still going. Although there were only a few people for the first few weeks, it quickly grew to between about seventeen and twenty-five. People stayed for varying times. Some came once or twice and decided it wasn't for them; others, however, stayed for years, some even for decades. At least a half-dozen came for so long that death was the only thing that stopped their continued attendance.

I was pressed to begin giving the *shiur* by a friend, but I refused for some time because I felt that I didn't know enough. My knowledge was much thinner than it is today,

## Australian Encounters

and I felt that it was dishonest to set myself up as a teacher in an area I was just discovering for myself.

But my friend was relentless and finally stymied me by suggesting I write to the Rebbe. I was actually pleased with the suggestion, because I figured the Rebbe would quickly veto the idea of an ignoramus watering down Jewish wisdom.

To my shock, this was not to be. I received a detailed reply: I was to conduct the *shiur*, but on condition that I prepared it carefully. Thirty-six years later, I can share that I have *never* given the *shiur* without preparing it thoroughly, in terror of the Rebbe's instruction. If I don't have the material on board by Sunday, I interrupt work on Monday to make sure I have it. What is now obvious to me is that the Rebbe, aware that the person who learns the most is the person giving the *shiur*, was simply helping me.

## TWO

Two or three years into the *shiur's* growth, a young doctor in his thirties, Tim Frank, began turning up. He knew little but was quietly excited by what he was learning, and because he was very intelligent, he absorbed a good deal quickly. He also asked me for reading lists and consumed them voraciously.

One Tuesday, we had a class on miracles. The Rebbe has explained that there are two kinds of miracles—those clothed in nature (and therefore not obvious) and those that interfere with nature (and are therefore obvious). This is not the place to explain the complexities of *Kabbalah* and Chasidut, but for this *shiur* I gave the example of a Sydney man who had some problem with his leg (I no longer remember what it was). After many doctors failed to help him, he wrote to the Rebbe, who told him to check his *mezuzot*. *Mezuzot* are parchments containing specific Torah wording, and they must be complete and whole when affixed to the doorpost. It turned out that in one of his *mezuzot*, the word in Hebrew for "walk" had a hole in it. The *mezuzah* was replaced and his leg soon recovered.

Even among the twenty or so people there that night, it was obvious to me that Tim was listening especially carefully. Sure enough, he stayed after the *shiur* and asked if he could speak to me.

The following sad story unfolded. Tim was happily married to a woman who taught secular studies in a Jewish school. Their happiness was compounded by beautiful twin boys, who would be bar mitzvah in a few years, prompting Tim to want to learn more about his heritage. Suddenly, disaster struck. His wife was diagnosed with cancer. Tim was beside himself, and he now wanted my opinion on whether he should go with his wife to see the Rebbe and ask for a *brachah*. I explained that although I give the *shiur*, I am not equipped to answer his question. I told him to ask a competent rabbi, although in my heart I wanted to tell him to get on the very next flight to New York!

## Australian Encounters

The following week, he stayed behind again and filled me in. He had asked the rabbi of the tiny synagogue he had started attending. This rabbi was young, passionate, and excited almost beyond reason by the Rebbe. He even went so far as to foolishly (in my opinion) guarantee Tim a miracle if only he went and believed with all his heart that the Rebbe could help them. As a result, Tim and his wife had sent the twins to stay with his parents, and they would be leaving for New York the next Sunday.

### THREE

At the time I had a deal with *shiur* members: If they went to the Rebbe, I would finish the *shiur* a little early, and the person would relate his experience and reactions to his moments with the Rebbe.

At the next *shiur* after Tim returned, I told him about our arrangement. Tim cleared his throat and told us hesitatingly that his trip to the Rebbe was one of the growth moments of his life. Standing before this angel (as he put it), whose blue eyes penetrated into his very soul, flooded him with warmth and security. The Rebbe gave him a dollar as well as one to his wife. When he told the Rebbe why he was there, the Rebbe wished his wife a "full recovery." Both he and his wife cherished the experience, but (and at this Tim cleared his throat) there was no *miracle*. Of course, they had more hope she would recover, but there was no miracle.

*chapter 8*

Almost as though he felt guilty, Tim assured everyone that going was an invaluable experience nonetheless.

As he was telling his story, his rabbi slipped in and quietly took up a standing position in the back. As he later told us, he wanted to hear Tim's impressions.

When Tim finished, the young rabbi muttered "impossible" under his breath repeatedly.

As the group dispersed, the rabbi asked Tim if he got a video. (All encounters with the Rebbe when he handed out dollars were filmed, and for a small charge one could buy a video of the precious moments). When Tim confirmed that they had, the rabbi asked if he could bring it to the *shiur* the following week so that the three of us could watch it together after the *shiur*.

## FOUR

We went upstairs to the TV and inserted the video.

As Tim had observed, there didn't seem to be anything remarkable. Tim told the Rebbe his wife's diagnosis slowly and clearly in exact medical terms, and he asked for a *brachah* that she would be well. The Rebbe handed Tim a dollar and wished his wife a full recovery. He then turned to Tim's wife, gave her a dollar, and repeated the blessing.

That was it.

"Play it again," the rabbi said. And then again, and then, again. I started getting restless.

Suddenly, after multiple playings, the rabbi jumped to his feet and yelled, "*There!*"

Suddenly, I saw it, too. Men and women line up separately for dollars. After giving the dollar to Tim, the Rebbe turned to the large group of women waiting for their turn. The Rebbe stretched out his hand into the second row and gave the dollar to Tim's wife while rearticulating the *brachah*.

"*How could he know that she was Tim's wife?!*"

Tim sat speechless. We played the video one last time, and the enormity of what had happened penetrated us all.

Crowds of thousands would line up for dollars from the Rebbe, men separately from women. The lines stretched from 770 Eastern Parkway and around the block. For the most part, the secretaries moved people briskly so that everyone could have their moment with the Rebbe. It was rare for a person to be introduced to the Rebbe. The video testified to the fact that there was no introduction to Tim, and more critically to his wife. Tim explained eloquently why he was there, but there was simply no way to connect him to his wife, who had been standing together with other women.

## FIVE

Tim continued attending the *shiur* for about five years.

My son has lived in Singapore until recently. It is the main synagogue's habit to host a dinner for all congregants on Friday night. For visitors, it is a lovely social event ensur-

*chapter 8*

ing convivial company at one's Shabbat dinner away from home.

On one of our visits to see our son a couple of years ago, we enjoyed eating our Shabbat meal with everyone in the synagogue. We were delighted to find that sitting next to us were Dr. Tim Frank and his wife, who were on their way to Europe. *Both* were healthy and happy, and after Shabbat they proudly showed us pictures of their grandchildren from both of the twins.

# Has He Seen My X-Rays?!

*chapter 9*

**ONE**

This story took place at some point between 1992 and 1993.

The Rebbe had his first stroke on 27 Adar I 1992 and a second on exactly the same date two years later.

Of course, we were all terribly shocked by the news. I was working in my office when Rabbi Feldman rang to tell me that the Rebbe had collapsed while at the Ohel. At that stage, there was no clear news. Slowly, we became aware of the seriousness of his condition. The range of reactions was vast; some said the Rebbe could (and would) fix himself in days, others said that he really didn't have a stroke and people were lying, still others were furiously trying to find a source in Scripture that this was the immediate sign of the coming of Mashiach.

Slowly but surely, a practical necessity began to emerge. What would happen to our communication with the Rebbe? To everyone's immense relief, it eventually became known that the Rebbe would continue to answer mail. However, since his speech was impaired, advice should be sought using alternatives. For example (and this is deliberately silly): "If I am to eat an apple, should it be

a. A red apple;
b. A green apple."

The Rebbe would then be able to communicate his answers to his secretaries by either nodding or shaking his head.

One more piece of information is relevant. Many of the letters we wrote (all handwritten on plain, unlined paper) were to a very large extent sent by fax—then an amazing new technology. The secretaries would pass them to the Rebbe, scrupulously jot down the Rebbe's exact reply, and then fax the answer back to the writer. Although initially rare, fax machines quickly proliferated in the workplace, and my office had one, as well.

## TWO

At that time, my mother-in-law was about seventy years old and generally in good health. She was vigorous and energetic, working as a full partner with my father-in-law in a

*chapter 9*

successful business. She allowed herself little downtime, and when she wasn't working, she devoted herself to various side activities with gusto.

In 1992, she felt unwell and presented with symptoms that her doctor suspected might be a brain tumor. She was sent for tests, and within days her fears were confirmed. Not only did she have the suspected tumor, it was huge—the size of a small orange.

The only treatment possible was major surgery. This would involve opening the scalp and carefully (and necessarily very precisely) cutting out the tumor. This was a daunting task for even the most experienced surgeon because of the sheer size of the tumor and its proximity to vital areas of the brain.

During the war years, my mother-in-law had apparently received some radiation treatment on her scalp (which was possibly the cause of the tumor). This earlier medical problem caused an independent issue—the skin on her scalp was dangerously thin and unlikely to heal if interfered with.

In short, surgery was a massive risk. To be successful, both hurdles had to be cleared. There was the considerable risk of collateral damage from the excision; equally dangerous, however, was the fact that if the skin on the scalp didn't heal, the brain could become quickly and irreparably infected.

On the other hand, without surgical intervention the prognosis was that she wouldn't survive for more than a year.

Death would be accompanied by considerable general suffering and pain.

My father-in-law arranged for her to be seen by the best neurological unit at one of the major teaching hospitals. A group of experts, including a neurologist, a neurosurgeon, and a plastic surgeon, held a lengthy joint meeting to assess the risk and make a recommendation. They determined that operating was not feasible. If the skin didn't heal, she could die a horribly painful death from infection, and if there was even the slightest inaccuracy with the excision of the tumor, she would be paralyzed and in a vegetative state.

Needless to say, the family was in deep shock. My father-in-law immediately set about obtaining a second opinion from an equally-venerable team at an equally-reputable teaching hospital. The decision was the same. Then he went for a third opinion, but they reached the same conclusion.

### THREE

My in-laws had two children—my wife and her younger sister.

I, however, am an only child. Growing up, I had almost no Jewish education. My parents, who were Holocaust survivors, shed their observance when they fled Europe. I found my way back to observance through Chabad. Happily, my wife, Ann, was a full partner in our journey. Her sister, Sandy, and her parents remained very much secular Jews, although sympathetic to our way of life. Inevitably, some small influ-

*chapter 9*

ences from our ways took hold, and Sandy grew accustomed to writing to the Rebbe for guidance. Much younger than Ann, marriage did nothing to strengthen her observance. However, she continued to write to the Rebbe.

So it was that, devastated by the thought of losing their mother, both women arrived at my office so they could send a fax to the Rebbe. Before writing, they sat with tears in their eyes as they discussed what exactly they should write. They determined that since they didn't have a question, there was therefore no need for alternatives, so they would just write for blessings. Finally, they determined that they should give a full account of the medical advice, and, since there wasn't going to be an operation, ask for a blessing that the short time their mother had left be pain-free and that she should die as comfortably as possible. After changing the wording a few times, they stood at the fax machine, and, choking back more tears, finally pressed the send button.

The two of them stayed for a bit. About a half-hour after they sent the fax, I was astonished when the phone rang on my desk and the receptionist announced that a Rabbi Groner was on the line. Of the Rebbe's secretaries, Rabbi Groner was my pathway to the Rebbe.

Rabbi Groner's familiar voice was grave and at the same time urgent. He told me that the Rebbe's reaction to the fax was so unusual that he didn't feel he could do it justice in a note. He wanted to impress upon me his account so that I could relay it accurately to my wife and her sister.

He told me that when he finished reading the letter to the Rebbe, the Rebbe became agitated and shook his head furiously. Rabbi Groner did not understand and asked what the Rebbe meant. After guessing wrongly a few times, he asked whether the Rebbe was saying that, contrary to the medical advice, my mother-in-law should go through with the operation. To this the Rebbe vigorously nodded his head. Conscious of the seriousness of the situation, Rabbi Groner asked again whether the Rebbe was saying that she should, in fact, be operated on and that the operation would be successful. Again, the Rebbe firmly nodded his head. Rabbi Groner felt the very strong reaction of the Rebbe and the emphasis expressed by him needed to be communicated verbally, hence the phone call.

I was, of course, very careful to communicate the content of the phone call to the women as accurately as possible.

## FOUR

Needless to say, they were both ecstatic. Hugging each other and laughing through new tears, they rushed off to deliver the wonderful news to their mother that her death sentence had been commuted to ongoing happy life!

It didn't occur to either of them to doubt the Rebbe's instruction in any way.

When they found their mother, they burst into an excited account of what had happened, each adding to the other's account until every detail had been remembered and com-

*chapter 9*

municated. Expecting their excitement to be shared by her, you can imagine how they felt when their mother replied, "Are you both mad?"

I was there and can testify that the silence was deafening. She continued, "Just because Ann has gone crazy religious with Robert, does that mean that you are also crazy, Sandy?"

Both sisters broke into tears.

"Mum, you are going to *live*! What are you talking about?!"

"What are *you* talking about," snapped my mother-in-law. "You want me to listen to a rabbi instead of a doctor? A team of doctors? *Three* teams of doctors from three of the best hospitals?"

"But Mum, it's the *Rebbe*!"

"So what? Has he seen my X-rays? Has he seen my blood tests?"

From her perspective, her logic was compelling. I tried to explain this to my wife and her sister as we stood outside their mother's house, but they were understandably inconsolable.

**FIVE**

My father-in-law was a man of wisdom and humility. Loved by all, his pathways were always peace and compromise. I doubt he believed in my mother-in-law's position any less than she, but, after all, this *was* from the Lubavitcher Rebbe.

He therefore proposed a compromise that was destined to be life changing—he suggested seeing another doctor.

My mother-in-law flatly refused. Understandably, she was tired of all of the exams. After three sets of MRIs, multiple X-rays, and innumerable blood tests, she had had enough. Finally, after many more tears and the girls pulling the "it's-not-fair-to-us" card, she relented.

A couple of days later, she was in front of a general practitioner—not even a specialist. He listened carefully, and when he was asked for his opinion, he truthfully replied that he didn't have the slightest idea. What he *could* suggest, and what he strongly recommended, was that she see a neurosurgeon named Besser. If anyone in the world could accurately assess the situation it was him, the doctor insisted. When my mother-in-law grudgingly agreed, he made the appointment on the spot and called in a favor to have it scheduled for the next day.

The next morning, my in-laws went to Dr. Besser's office together with all the test results.

Dr. Besser took his time examining the MRIs, X-rays, and bloodwork. Then he said quietly, "I really don't see the problem. I routinely do more complicated surgery, and the danger of the scalp not healing is vastly exaggerated."

## SIX

Dr. Besser operated, the procedure went like clockwork, the skin healed, and my mother-in-law lived for more than

## chapter 9

twenty years afterward, passing away when she was in her early nineties.

However, this can't just be a nice story with a happy ending. There are some very important questions anyone hearing this story must ask themselves.

Who could possibly have given advice like the Rebbe did?

How could he give it? Who could take such responsibility?

The question is strengthened by my mother-in-law's plaintive objection: **Has he seen my X-rays? Has he seen my blood tests?**

Regardless of how little strangers may know of the Rebbe, no one would dare suggest irresponsibility from the Moses of our generation. The only answer consistent with any level of responsibility is that the Rebbe *knew*.

How he knew is beyond all my horizons. I'm just telling you the story…

# A Very Curious Exchange
*chapter 10*

It is trite to remark that we are all different. Some have a flair for certain things, others for others. Conversely, some people find it difficult to do things that their friends find easy.

I have no talent for languages. Some people learn a new language as easily as acquiring a new suit, but for me, how they do it is a total mystery.

When I began to learn Torah some forty years ago, there wasn't much available in English. It seems incredible considering the vastness of books and resources in English today, but it was so. I soon realized that I needed Hebrew in order to learn Torah. This was even more necessary for learning Chasidut.

## Australian Encounters

I began to learn for a half-hour every day with a friend, Meyer Moss, who is blessed with the flair for language completely lacking in me. Our system was that I read the Hebrew word, and he translated it. The idea was that sooner or later I would begin to remember the vocabulary, thus slowly learning the language. The system was good, the student weak. With kind patience, he tolerated my bumbling, slow progress. We learned day after day, and finally, after a long time, I was able to follow when someone else read. Ultimately, I was able to learn alone. I am forever indebted to him for his patience. (Indeed, what then developed naturally into a *shiur* between us lasted almost thirty years.)

When I learned my first *maamar* (Chasidic discourse) alone, I was so excited that I wrote to the Rebbe to share my elation. I had finally arrived as a Hebrew understander!

As usual at that time, I received no reply.

Years passed.

The first time I went to the Rebbe for dollars was a unique experience. As anyone who experienced dollars will testify, the moment with the Rebbe can be overwhelming. The emotions are a cholent of anticipation, anxiety, pleasure, and an enormous sense of growth.

The Rebbe's blue eyes bored into my soul. As I discovered later, this was always the case. But the Rebbe also broke into a warm smile and then spoke a few sentences. I had absolutely no idea what he said, and I was shuffled along to make room for the next person. I tried to deal with the mixed

*chapter 10*

emotions. On the one hand, the moment was awe-inspiring; on the other hand, I hadn't understood anything that the Rebbe had said.

By Divine Providence, the person after me in the queue was also from Australia. Rabbi Y. Barber, a friend for many years, had heard what the Rebbe had said to me. He came over to me in the bustling crowd that collects after one is moved on and remarked that it had been a very curious exchange. When I asked what he meant, he observed that the Rebbe had spoken to me in *Lashon Kodesh* (the Hebrew of Scripture).

As I said, I didn't understand a single word. At the same time, I now understood everything.

I didn't explain it to my friend, mentally cherishing the intimacy of the moment with the Rebbe, but the Rebbe's communication to me was completely clear.

Incredibly, the Rebbe was acknowledging my letter from so many years earlier! Additionally, I flushed at the degree to which my boast was kindly shown to me as premature. Finally, I accepted the implication to do more with my Hebrew.

How the Rebbe could remember the letter containing such trivia from a Jew across the world for so many years is totally bewildering. How he knew to instantly bring it to mind and communicate it is, for me, nothing short of miraculous.

# The Video

*chapter 11*

**ONE**

On one of our trips to the Rebbe, when our son Akiva was about eight years old, there happened to be a children's rally organized in front of the Rebbe. The *shul* at 770 Eastern Parkway was packed with children and parents vainly trying to keep some sort of order before the rally began. Suddenly, the Rebbe entered, flanked by two of his secretaries, and walking with his customary briskness. There was instant silence. A path suddenly appeared from nowhere, and then everyone froze. I remember marveling at how, without a word of admonition or warning, hundreds of children stood in awe as the Rebbe strode quickly to his place through the newly created pathway.

## Australian Encounters

Rabbi JJ Hecht was the MC, smoothly practiced at the task.

Part of the program, indeed a highlight, was the recitation of the Twelve *Pesukim*. (Chabad children are taught to say the Twelve *Pesukim*—which are a collection of verses, Talmudic aphorisms, and phrases from *Tanya*—by heart from a young age.)

I don't remember how, but somehow it was arranged for Akiva, together with Dovey Barber—Akiva's classmate from Sydney—to recite one of the verses together out loud, with the other children repeating it after them. Rabbi Hecht made much of announcing in a very important sounding voice that the next verse would be recited by two boys who had come all the way from Sydney, Australia!

In case the reader has never seen it, the method is for the child to hold up an outstretched arm and loudly recite the verse.

Rabbi Hecht thrust the microphone at Akiva, who grabbed it eagerly. Both boys, totally unrehearsed, screamed their verse into the microphone while waving their respective arms with great vigor. I was torn between looking at the boys while brimming with pride and looking at the Rebbe—and feeling equally proud as I registered his broad smile of enjoyment and approval.

Thankfully, the whole episode is on video, and we have a copy, which is one of our precious possessions.

*chapter 11*

## TWO

Akiva was thirteen at the time of the Rebbe's passing. Like many children, it took time for this to register—in fact, it took many years. When he was in his twenties—again, like many young adults—Akiva's attention to his observance weakened. He remained observant, of course, but his vigilance and passion began to wane.

Everyone handles things differently, and the method of maintaining a connection with the Rebbe is no different. Some do so by studying the Rebbe's teachings, some by sending letters to the Ohel (the Rebbe's gravesite), and some by other means. I know one holy Jew who goes to the *mikveh*, puts on his Shabbat clothes and a *gartel*, and then sits down with his eyes closed as he talks to the Rebbe out loud.

Akiva's business life involves constant traveling. When he has business to negotiate, his preference is to do so face to face, so he usually just gets on a plane to meet his prospective business colleague.

So it was that when Akiva needed advice from the Rebbe, he jumped on a plane and visited the Ohel in person.

Slowly, he found that this was happening with less and less frequency. He began to have doubts about Chabad "without" a Rebbe—was the Rebbe becoming just a picture on the wall? Was there really a level of communication that could justify the time and money to travel from Asia (where he was based) to New York? If his relationship with the Rebbe had contracted by the Rebbe's passing, what was the point of making the lengthy trip?

## THREE

We are close, and Akiva decided to discuss it with me. I suggested to Akiva that he had to pick a lane. If the Rebbe was his Rebbe, why not tell him? Why not ask his advice as he had done regarding all the other matters in his life? On the other hand, anything less was an admission that the Rebbe was no longer his Rebbe. Had he really come to that?

Akiva decided to go. He arrived in Brooklyn and arranged for a car service to take him to the Ohel. He did not make any attempt to formalize the visit by going to the *mikveh* or even changing his clothing.

What he did do when it was his turn to go in was pour his heart out. He needed help from the Rebbe. He needed to know he was still there for him, and lonely as it was without him, it had to be real. If it wasn't real for Akiva, it was of no value. Then Akiva surprised himself by asking for a sign. He felt guilty asking, but he needed one; he wanted something that would give him some level of assurance of the Rebbe's real presence. He then recited some chapters of Psalms and then left after repeating his tearful request for a sign.

Outside the Ohel there is an adjacent building where people can prepare before entering and rest after leaving. Akiva looked around for his driver, but he saw that he was praying the *Minchah* service, which is short, so he decided to wait without disturbing him.

In the building there are screens that play videos of the Rebbe on a constant basis, and visitors are welcome to watch at their leisure.

Since he was waiting anyway, Akiva sat down at a table to watch the video.

He nearly fainted.

There, at that exact moment, was a replay of him as a little boy screaming his verse while the Rebbe looked on intently, smiling broadly.

Akiva had his sign! Of all the thousands of hours of video material on the Rebbe, even the most hardened skeptic could not possibly contend this to be a coincidence. What are the odds that a man cries to his Rebbe for communication and is suddenly given a palpable hug in response?!

## FOUR

The story has an epilogue. There was a young *yeshivah* student sitting on the bench next to Akiva at the same table. He witnessed the whole episode.

Understandably, when Akiva immediately rang his wife to share the miracle, he wanted some private time with what had happened so he could come to terms with it and its implications. He therefore asked her not to tell anyone. He needn't have bothered. By the time he got off the plane in

## Australian Encounters

Asia, the young student had posted news of the miracle on a Chabad site and the whole world knew.

Akiva says that the Rebbe must have wanted the episode publicized.

Today, Akiva and that student, who is now a rabbi, are friends, and Akiva helps him with his Chabad House.

Most importantly, Akiva has a Rebbe.

# The Machne Israel Result
*chapter 12*

**ONE**

Sometime in 1987, I received a phone call from Rabbi Feldman asking me to meet with him. After the usual pleasantries, he told me that there was a kind of club in existence that I should consider joining. Carefully and fairly slowly, he outlined its background and conditions.

Machne Israel is one of the Rebbe's institutions; it is devoted to caring for the social and religious welfare of Jews around the world. In order to support it financially, the Rebbe brought together a group of philanthropists to form the Machne Israel Development Fund. The Rebbe had offered participation in this group on the basis of donations from incumbent members in return for private audiences

## Australian Encounters

with him. The cost for this was $100,000 US, payable over five years—$20,000 per year, in two payments of $10,000, with one due before Pesach and the other during the Hebrew month of Tishrei. Participants could have a private audience twice a year—during those same time periods. Over the previous decade, the Rebbe had stopped giving private audiences to all but extremely few people, and to have private time with the Rebbe was an enormous and self-evident privilege. Rabbi Feldman told me that when he said I should participate, he wasn't just speaking as my rabbi but also as my friend, because in his opinion, I could afford it.

Sometimes in life a good deal of thought seems to occupy a small amount of time. Although it took place so long ago, I remember my thought process as clearly as if it took place last week. There were a few parts to my thinking, and the reader will surely recognize that sometimes all thoughts seem to come at once.

First, the Australian dollar was about seventy-five cents to the US dollar at the time, which meant that the cost was about $130,000 Australian. For context, a house in Sydney that is now worth $15 million would have cost about $500,000 back then. So the equivalent in today's money would be about four million dollars, payable over five years. Rabbi Feldman might have thought that I could afford it, but I couldn't see how.

Second, and more importantly, I was honestly deeply shocked. I had come to Chabad to escape the shallow drives

*chapter 12*

of self-interest that I had witnessed in the general community. Here, in Chabad, I was learning life lessons that I saw as supremely valuable. The focus was on learning how to serve G-d, to learn His commandments, and to perform them. In doing so, a Jew had the opportunity to change the world for the better, and I was proud to be training to be part of this process. Spearheading all this was the Rebbe, who was the unquestioned intellectual, moral, and spiritual giant guiding the perfecting of the world, one action at a time, one person at a time.

And now this was to be tainted by money?

This is what I had so desperately wanted to leave behind. I wanted to leave the places where money not only talked but was the only language. I wanted to exchange that language for truth, justice, and everything noble about which I was learning. Suddenly I felt like I was being invited back into the sewer, and worse, by the Rebbe himself! There were fine men in this new religious community to which I was beginning to belong; there were rabbis and scholars whom I admired. They couldn't have a private audience with the Rebbe; they could hardly afford the airfare, let alone the vast amount of money for the fund! Yet Kremnizer, ignorant of everything important, could have a private audience, not once, but ten times, and why? Because he could pay?!

Was this what I had sacrificed for? Holy men couldn't have a private audience, but *I* could if I paid enough?

I became conscious of Rabbi Feldman looking at me. He

remarked that I had not said anything. One of the strengths of our relationship—and this is entirely to his credit, because it is not so with other people—is that I have never felt inhibited to share my inner feelings with him.

I told him what I was thinking. I didn't do it gently; rather, I expressed the emotion that had welled up in me. I told him in detail how deeply disappointed I was to witness another fleecing process after thinking that Chabad was an island apart from the grasping hypocrisy that justified an unwanted hand in one's pocket.

Rabbi Feldman sat quietly for a few moments; there was silence between us.

Then, choosing his words carefully, he explained kindly that one of the big obstacles on the mountain I was trying to climb was ego. A moment's serious thought, he continued, would show that I was using my own opinions to judge the Rebbe. He believed that as soon as I realized this, I would find it comical. The Rebbe was the Rebbe. He wasn't held in the highest esteem for nothing. This was the Rebbe's system, and that being so, it must be for the good. Kremnizer's opinion was only held up by the hot air of ego. Since I had come this far, why not abdicate my ego, recognize that this was the Rebbe's system, and do what I could to be part of it?

His words must have been well chosen, because I suddenly saw the shallowness of my reaction. I trusted the Rebbe with my health and children, but I was suddenly balking at money?

*chapter 12*

To preserve my options, I said that I would think about it, but as I got up to leave, I knew that I had already made up my mind.

## TWO

The first private audience my wife, Ann, and I had was not the first time we had met the Rebbe. Having said that, this was entirely different. I described the public talk in Chapter 6. The private time with the Rebbe involved matters too personal to report here. Suffice it to say that Ann started shaking nervously, then melted into tears, and then slowly but surely steadied herself until she was obviously filled with confidence and optimism. The Rebbe answered my question second, and I have hung onto that answer ever since.

I have to share that, somehow, every Pesach and every Tishrei, the money for the payment materialized. I don't remember ever being able to plan the next payment, but somehow it was always there, and I was never late.

The incredible thing to which I must admit was how blasé we were about it. The Rebbe's passing was unthinkable. Of the number of times we were entitled to go to New York, we only went a few times! Instead, we sent others; once it was my mother and her husband, sometimes it was friends, and on one occasion we missed it simply because it was unmanageable. I was busy, the children had things on, parent obligations were in the way, etc. What a travesty! If we had the opportunity today…

Incidentally, I learned how right Rabbi Feldman had been that day in his office. The Machne Israel Development Fund was essentially a businessmen's club. It was not an environment for receiving blessings that poor people couldn't access. The Rebbe decided that it was time for some wealth in Chabad, and how is wealth created? Through charity. Far from being exploited, the participants were unknowingly being kissed by the Rebbe, who was steering them through a Torah constant to the wealth they themselves wanted. Blessings for health and children and all forms of advancement, spiritual or physical, remained obviously available to all through letters and Sunday Dollars, when the Rebbe handed out dollars to the thousands who queued for hours at designated times.

## THREE

In 1990, Australia went into the recession "it had to have," courtesy of then-Prime Minister Keating. I had built up a large property portfolio with two partners. This is not the place to explain, but in essence my partners' external interests caused the need to sell our prime property into a panicked and falling market. The positive cash flow from these properties had been servicing debt that had been deliberately incurred to protect against taxes, and as the properties were sold, this positive cash flow was steadily extinguished. The debt, however, remained, and slowly but surely the money to service this separate debt was being progressively strangled as each property was sold.

This draining process took two years, and by 1992 I was facing the real prospect of bankruptcy.

In March of 1992 (on 27 Adar I), the Rebbe suffered his first stroke. Without getting into the reactions we all had, I will simply note that I had just made the Pesach payment, and life continued with the new and growing focus on the Rebbe's health.

## FOUR

As the year continued, my position kept getting worse. And, as life had it, September (the next and final payment) came quickly. I don't remember the exact reason, but a couple of weeks before this last payment was due to be paid, we were holidaying in Surfers Paradise, Queensland. My in-laws owned an apartment there, and, at my wife's suggestion, I was taking a week's break from the pressure cooker my office had become.

Walking on the beach alone, I was thinking of the looming payment. My office was fueled by an overdraft, and I can still remember the numbers twenty-eight years later. I needed about 13,000 Australian dollars for the payment. My overdraft limit was such that after the payment I would only have enough overhead for about three weeks.

Then what? Closure? Bankruptcy?

Suddenly, I realized what a smart lawyer I was. I re-

## Australian Encounters

viewed the deal. I had pledged $100,000 over five years for the private audiences, and since there wouldn't be any this year that meant that I didn't have to pay!

My heart leaped at my genius and the sudden windfall of $13,000.

I hurried home to tell my wife and ring Rabbi Feldman (those were the days before mobile phones were prevalent).

Ann was out shopping, so I rang Rabbi Feldman. He knew my position, because I had shared with him every landslide on the way down the slope of losses.

Triumphantly, I explained my brilliant legal analysis. I was paying for something that wasn't available; therefore, clearly, I didn't have to pay.

Good friends know one another's body language even over the phone. Rabbi Feldman was silent. I was concerned, so I invited him to agree with me. More silence.

Finally, Rabbi Feldman said that he didn't understand. I had turned my whole life around for what to me was a new belief system. I had taken my eldest child out of a secular school, notwithstanding my family's condemnation for experimenting with her life. I had enrolled all subsequent children into the same Jewish school. My wife and I had uprooted our lives—kosher, Shabbat, family purity. We had trusted the Rebbe's advice about health, our children, and their education. Now, at the last moment, at the last gasp, I was going to give up?

And what if it had all been a mistake? What if it had

all been for nothing? What if my legal argument had some value? He pointed out that I would just be bankrupt a couple of weeks earlier.

As I put down the phone, I kept $13,000 worth of gloom at bay by resolving to discuss all this as planned with Ann.

My wife listened to the lawyer but answered the husband.

"Pay it—but happily!"

## FIVE

I arranged the money transfer the next day.

Today, so many years later, things have rectified themselves, thank G-d.

I state in all solemnity that our financial recovery began on that very day, and I never reached that overdraft limit. I can't identify any specific miraculous event that flowed from this moment other than the general reality that up until that day I had been staring down the road to bankruptcy, and from that day forward the pressures began to relax. Day by day, week by week, more and more things fell into place, and within half a year or so not only were we out of danger, but real positive opportunities began to flourish.

# For Some People There Are No Questions, for Some People There Are No Answers

*chapter 13*

### ONE

I don't remember where and how I met Peter Hoffman. However, I liked him very much from the first time I met him. To say that his was a complex personality is a wild understatement. He was a cocktail of conflicting energies, and although this may not have endeared him to all, I found him both stimulating and exasperating at the same time.

The forum for our friendship was the tennis court. We have a tennis court at home (which we share with a neighbor). Throughout the '80s and '90s, I played about three times a week. My tennis was very average, and considering my passion for the game and the hundreds of hours of practice, the standard I reached was unremarkable.

## Australian Encounters

Any reader who plays will testify that tennis is one of those endeavors where equality between the players is helpful. In other words, playing someone either well below or well above one's standard does not make for either a good workout or a pleasurable game.

I was always on the lookout for partners who were on my level. Once I found such a person, I tried to establish a regular game to avoid the constant searching.

So it was that Peter became my Thursday afternoon partner; we played together every week throughout the '80s and into the '90s. Playing with Peter had three advantages: He was never late, our scores were very equal, and the postgame chats over a cool drink were stimulating. Stimulating, but often maddening at the same time.

### TWO

The reason the chats were maddening was that Peter always wanted to talk about religion. No matter what I did to change the subject, he always brought the conversation back to Judaism in general and observance in particular. This on its own could have been the best subject possible, but there was a problem. He had appointed himself the critic of everything Jewish, and his denigrations were fiercely intended to be destructive. Early on in our relationship I would fall into his traps, because his method of criticism was to couch his condemnation in a question. The question would be carefully framed so that any answer I would give would become the

*chapter 13*

springboard for his censure. I tired of this quickly and pointed out that his questions were not questions but answers that he wanted to justify. To be fair to him, he accepted the truth of this and thereafter his attacks were at least more honest. For a long time I took him seriously. I wanted to influence him positively, and because he simply would not leave the subject alone, I spent hours trying to convince him of the shallowness of his perspectives. Ultimately, when I realized that I couldn't help him, I started working harder to just change the subject so I could be rid of the burden.

Peter was a good deal older than me. We started playing tennis together when I was about forty, and he was then in his mid-sixties, although he was in very good shape. He had retired at forty, having sold his large printing business for a small fortune, and then through canny (or lucky) investments, he had succeeded in converting the small fortune into a large one. He spent his retirement looking after his body with rigid food and exercise regimes. Part of his recreation time was spent fishing with a regular partner. Every Wednesday, they would set out before it was light and spend the day in a small rowboat with an outboard motor, which they moored at different spots in the harbor. Peter and his wife ate a lot of fish, which Peter was fond of saying cost him nothing.

At the time when we began to play, his three children were already adults.

Extraordinarily, two of the three had found their way

to Chabad! His second child, a daughter, married a young Chabad man and kept a Chabad home with many children. His youngest, a son, was then away studying in a Chabad *yeshivah*. Peter saw it as one of life's great ironies that two-thirds of his offspring were "*meshuga frum*" (crazy religious). Although I know his wife was very proud of this, to this day I am still uncertain if Peter not only secretly approved but maybe was himself proud, despite his protestations. In any event, his outward demeanor was that of a scoffer, made more influential to the unwary by his polite pretense at respect while actually trying to turn the knife.

## THREE

In the beginning of 1987, there was great celebration in Chabad. This is not the place for a description; suffice it to say that after a court case, stolen books were returned to Chabad. At that time, the Rebbe explained something extraordinary: The victory was a spiritual one, as well as a physical one, and it was an opportune time to ask the Almighty for anything one needed. The Rebbe encouraged us to ask for whatever we wanted, because it was a moment in time when our requests would be answered! Can you imagine?

For those who couldn't get a note to the Rebbe, some went to pray at the gravesite of a *tzaddik*.

One such person was Peter's son-in-law, Yanky. This was a Thursday morning, and before he went he stopped off at the home of his in-laws and excitedly explained the unique opportunity to Peter. He could ask for anything he wanted! To his utter amazement, Peter refused. Peter felt that it was all nonsense, and he wasn't going to change his belief system on some whim that didn't make sense to him. Yanky pointed out that Peter could ask for health, wealth, and *nachat* from his children and grandchildren. Smugly, Peter pointed out that he was in excellent health, rich, and happy with his children and grandchildren, so he had everything he needed.

Finally, feeling sorry for his son-in-law, Peter said that he would make a request, after all. He told Yanky to ask that his next fishing outing be hugely successful.

Yanky was close to tears of frustration, but he was able to tell himself not to be upset. To his credit, he did make Peter's request when he prayed at the gravesite.

That afternoon, I was horrified when Peter told me the story. He was completely without regret at the travesty, and the only impression the episode had made on him was that he was looking forward to fishing the following Wednesday.

### FOUR

The next Thursday Peter was very quiet. Additionally, he played particularly badly. He was clearly preoccupied, and I never know whether it's helpful to intrude when friends don't volunteer their thoughts. After the game, I decided to ask whether he was alright. His response was somber and deliberate. He told me he had been given pause. Before I could ask what that meant, he explained that a good catch for him was usually between seven and ten fish. There was much rivalry between Peter and Jim (his fishing partner) over who would catch the most fish on a given day. Yesterday they went fishing as usual. Peter now lowered his voice and, clearly distraught, tremblingly told me that Jim had caught one solitary fish while he had caught one hundred and sixty-seven! After some silence, he repeated that it gave him pause.

I said nothing. The pain of the missed opportunity didn't need to be increased or highlighted. Peter had asked for a miracle and received it. The problem was that he had wasted the once-in-a-lifetime opportunity on foolishness. Peter went home clearly unhappy, and I felt very sorry for him.

## FIVE

The next week, Peter was his usual smiling self, and he assured me that he was back to normal. Again, I kept silent, but it didn't take long for an explanation. Peter had decided to check the tides and discovered that there had been a natural warm current in the direction that his boat was facing, and given his position in the boat it was logical that he would catch the fish. The fact that Jim had only caught one was due to where he was sitting. As to the astronomical amount of fish that he had caught, well, he was just on his game on a good day...

I remember sadly reviewing the well-known adage that *For some people there are no questions, and for some people there are no answers.*

# The Scam

*chapter 14*

**ONE**

To call someone simple carries with it an implication of cruelty. However, the only way I can describe Boris Kloptarsky truthfully—and without any intended cruelty whatsoever—is to observe that he is simple. Huge, broad, and heavy, he gave the impression of being twice his size, and he moved like a lumbering, kindly giant.

I met him back in the days when I had a general practice. He was a useful and pleasant client. His repeat business included some property transfers, probating quite a respectably-sized estate, and some immigration work for relatives whom he brought to Australia from his native Russia.

He somehow heard about my Tuesday night *shiur* and

became an invariably punctual attendee for some years. He always sat at the "back" (the end of the table furthest from me) and listened with the benign half-smile of someone happy but understanding almost nothing. He reminded me of a large contented dog happily nestled at the end of the family bed, sublimely unaware of most of the content of the conversation in the room.

He loved to be present, but based on conversations we had in the office, I was sure that he understood very little.

One thing that seemed to penetrate his smiling haze, however, was any information about the Rebbe. He loved to hear about the Rebbe, and his level of participation in the *shiur* visibly changed whenever I mentioned him. Boris would come alive and even ask questions. Finally, without telling me (which would have allowed me to make arrangements for someone to help him there), he went to New York to see the Rebbe for Sunday Dollars, and he returned ecstatic. He described the experience (in his limited vocabulary) as life-changing for him, and it was obvious to anyone that it was so. Simple or not, in the area of the Rebbe, his deeply sincere love for him was not only moving but inspiring.

## TWO

The time was the late '80s. Because it was so long ago, and probably also because I (thankfully) have a limited mental capacity for criminal scams, I don't remember the details of the racket I am about to describe. However, in

*chapter 14*

broad brushstrokes, it involved car theft. The owner of the car would leave his car parked with the keys inside, and a driver would collect the car and drive it out of the state. Once the owner was advised that the car had arrived (usually the next day—let's call it day two), the owner would report the loss to the police. He would report that the theft had occurred on day two, not the real date, day one, thus ensuring the car, which was now far away, could not be matched with the theft. Once the police realized that they couldn't find the car, a claim would be made to the insurance company, and all participating cheats were enriched.

Boris' car was stolen. He had left the keys inside, and to no one's surprise the car vanished. To this day, I believe that Boris had no idea that the scam explained above existed, let alone participated in it. Nevertheless, after reporting the theft to the police (and this is where my memory is hazy), when he made the insurance claim, the dates were different by one day. On one of the reports he had day one, on the other day two.

## THREE

The insurance company's records were matched by computer with the police reports, and the insurance company understandably thought that Boris was part of this well-known racket. They reported the matter to the DPP (Department of Public Prosecutors), and Boris was charged with fraud, which carried a sentence of five to ten years in prison.

Boris was beside himself, of course. How would he provide for his wife and two young children? How could the police be so wrong? What were they talking about anyway? How could this happen in Australia? This wasn't Communist Russia!

I felt sorry for him, because I believed that he had simply made a mistake. However, I explained that I didn't do criminal law, and I offered to introduce him to an acquaintance who was skilled in this area. Boris thanked me, but he said that he didn't need it because he had access to the solicitor used by his in-laws, and he would go to him. When he mentioned his name, I was horrified. The man he mentioned was a scurrilous crook who would doubtless milk poor Boris dry. He was an expert in unnecessary delays and all the other methodologies unscrupulous lawyers use to bring the profession into bad repute.

I asked Boris for a day to think about it, but providing I could get a specific barrister, Simon Gordon (see Chapter 2), I had made up my mind to take up the case, if only to save poor Boris from further violation.

A few days later, we were sitting in Simon Gordon's chambers, and he asked Boris to tell him the story in his own words. Poor, simple Boris looked at me for help, but he stumbled through the few short sentences on his own. He had parked in the street because his wife's car had been in their driveway. He must have left his keys in the car (he wasn't sure), and when he went outside the next day, his car was gone, so he went to the police. No car. No story. No real understanding of why he was here. When questioned by Simon as to the date disparity in the two reports, Boris simply didn't know how it had happened.

When he finished, Simon looked at me steadily and finally summed the matter up succinctly, observing that it was a simple case: It would depend entirely on whether the jury would believe that Boris was negligent but truthful, without any criminal involvement or guilt of attempted fraud.

Even Boris understood that his chances were looking poor, and I left Simon's chambers with a miserable lumbering giant.

In the taxi on the way home Boris suddenly brightened. "Would *my* Rebbe help me?"

I remember smiling to myself that the Rebbe had become *his*.

"I could ask for a *brachah*," he continued.

"Absolutely," I said.

We returned to my office, where Boris wrote a letter to the Rebbe in Russian. The next day I phoned him to tell him we had received a faxed reply.

Boris was back in the office at great speed. He collected the fax from me and took it to his rabbi, and he later phoned me excitedly to tell me that he had the Rebbe's *brachah*.

## FOUR

Jury selection is tedious for lawyers. Happily, in this case things went smoothly without challenges, and the case got underway very quickly. The Crown prosecutor outlined the case by first describing the general scam and then trying to show that Boris was culpable.

No sooner had the prosecutor described the way the scam worked when our world fell apart. One juror burst out laughing. He continued to laugh as each step was described, even digging his elbow into his neighbor's ribs while spluttering. How could we not have challenged him? On second look, he was quite dirty and disheveled. His laughter revealed a black hole where he was missing a tooth in the front of his mouth, and his fingernails were black with dirt. On the ear away from us and until now unseen, a silver earing completed the picture.

Clearly, he knew all about this scam. Implicit in his body language was that all of his friends knew of the scam, as well, doubtless being involved themselves. His face said it all: Boris was just another foreigner who was yanking the system, and he, the juror, was way too smart to let him get away with it.

At the end of the first day, Boris had still not given evidence, so the trial was extended to the next day.

Back in Simon's chambers, the miserable look on his face spoke eloquently. Our only chance to win was to get the jury to believe Boris' story, but it was clear that this juror would see to it that this would never happen.

I looked over at Boris. This huge figure sitting on a chair

that looked like it would break under him was motionless, with a benign smile fixed on his face. I tried to explain the gravity of our position, but Boris was unmoved, absolutely secure in his total belief in the Rebbe's *brachah*. The Rebbe had given his *brachah*; the trial was now *his* worry!

As we shook hands to leave, Simon's face was again eloquent. Our client may have a *brachah*, but there was no way he was getting out of this.

### FIVE

The next day, the judge didn't enter the court immediately, nor did the jury.

Instead, the lawyers were called to the judge's chambers. There, the judge explained that something unusual had happened and we had an option to consider.

One of the jurors had broken his leg overnight and would not be able to return to court. The defendant now had to decide whether to continue the trial one juror short or have a new trial called. The judge was not interested in hearing from the lawyers without instructions.

Simon was so happy that he almost danced from the judge's chambers. What a break! All the damage the juror had done wouldn't be there in a new trial! With a brand new jury, there was hope that they would believe Boris' story. How great to be able to get a new trial!

We went to the conference room, and Simon smilingly shared the wonderful news with Boris.

## Australian Encounters

Boris was quiet. Finally, he asked whether he would have to pay for *this* trial? "Of course," Simon spluttered, "but don't you understand the enormity of your good fortune?" Simon now looked at me for support, clearly concluding that Boris was not only simple but perhaps a little mad.

Then Boris said, "But what if it's *him*?"

"What?!"

"Well, what if it's *him* who broke his leg?"

I thought Simon was going to have a heart attack. He looked at me for confirmation that Boris needed certification, but then he changed his tone to one of kindness usually reserved for dumb animals.

"Boris, there is a one in twelve chance that it's him. That's just an eight percent chance. Please understand that this means that there is a ninety-two percent chance that it isn't him. Are you seriously considering those odds?! The risk is prison!"

Boris sat smiling happily.

"Mr. Gordon, I know you mean well, and I know it is not the money for a second trial that makes you tell me this, but I have a *brachah* from the Rebbe."

"What?!"

"I have a *brachah* from the Rebbe," he repeated.

I marveled at the energies in the room. Boris was so happy. Simon apoplectic.

"So I will go on with this trial."

Simon called me outside and shared our danger. His

*chapter 14*

position was that it was one thing for Boris to be insane, but we were vulnerable to a lawsuit if we didn't look after ourselves. Simon drafted a simple but clear release form explaining that we had recommended a new trial, that Boris was going against our advice, and that he alone was choosing to continue.

Boris signed the release and lumbered into court behind us, smiling happily.

## SIX

The judge ordered the resumption of the case, and we all stood as he entered the court. The jury was recalled. Simon wore his funeral face. My heart was in my mouth. The jurors entered one by one, and each time it wasn't the enemy, like Russian roulette, increasing the odds for the next one to be him.

Eleven!

No earing!

I couldn't believe it.

The rest of the trial went like a knife through butter. Simon's cross-examination took long enough for the jurors to conclude the truth. Boris was simple, he didn't understand many of the questions until they were explained multiple times, but he had not defrauded anyone.

## SEVEN

In the cab back to the office, I felt a sudden lump in my

throat when Boris said simply, "When we get back to your office, I am going to write to say thank you to *my* Rebbe."

# Rain

*chapter 15*

**ONE**

Before I begin this story, I must disclose a male defect. In an age of political correctness, I know it is dangerous to isolate a gender and generalize, but in my experience, I am not alone among men in this defect.

I just don't understand weddings. At least I don't understand extravagant weddings. I freely admit that I don't get why struggling parents have to get into serious debt to marry off a child. I don't understand why the huge amount of money involved couldn't be better spent on a deposit for a home. I don't see why so many industries need servicing by the poor and bewildered soon-to-be-further-impoverished parents. And to be clear, entire industries have mushroomed to feed off these weddings. Flowers, gowns, hall, band, caterers, waiters, and even cars in some instances. Why?

How is this going to help the young couple?

How is this going to add to the *simchah* of the parents (unless they are not paying)?

The very sad predicate is that somehow there has arisen enormous social pressure to match (and even in some cases outdo) the last friend's wedding, with more people, better food, and even take-away presents. Indeed, if the last wedding's table centerpieces were nice, the next have to be marvelous, and the mother of the bride or groom are somehow less deserving of respect if the centerpieces don't match up.

## TWO

Our eldest daughter got engaged with the Rebbe's *brachah* on the day before Sukkot, 1991. The wedding was set for Sunday, December 15, of that year. To my gasping relief, my father-in-law offered to pick up the tab for the wedding in its entirety. Nicky was our first to marry, and she was also the first grandchild to marry. To my father-in-law, a wedding with searchlights and elephants was mandatory for his first adored grandchild.

## THREE

I spent some time in solitude, formulating a wonderful plan. Wouldn't it be a great thing for our community if we took the opportunity to turn this all on its head? If people like us, who were known not to have to compete financially for misplaced status, had a simple wedding, couldn't others follow the example without embarrassment? If we had a small dinner and then welcomed anyone who wanted to join us (with their own bottle) to dance the night away, not only could we have a wonderful wedding, but it would set a precedent that had not been spawned from an inability to spend the money. Everyone could subscribe to the wisdom of the new paradigm without having to be judged on the money they were spending. The religious community in Sydney was generally poor, but no one needed the hosts' piece of chicken, and everyone could invest in each other's future happy occasions without the tyranny of the expense.

I felt elated when I went home to share my wisdom with Ann.

**FOUR**

"Are you crazy?!"

Ann looked at me in shocked disbelief.

"Does our poor daughter have to be the victim of your ill-considered plans?"

I was about to defend myself, sure that I hadn't explained my genius idea properly, when Ann continued, "Please, I don't want to hear this again. Nicky is over the moon about the wedding, Daddy and Mom are over the moon about the wedding, your mother and Max are over the moon about the wedding, *and so are we!*"

Every husband, even at his dumbest, knows when he has reached a line that can't be crossed.

"In fact," Ann added with continued firmness, "we would all be grateful if you would stay out of all the arrangements and just let us do our thing."

From Gladiator for the Poor to Silenced Husband in about forty-three seconds…

### FIVE

The wedding approached with speed, but not too fast for Ann to weave her magic. Flowers, gowns, hall, band, caterers, waiters, cars, all arranged according to Ann's good-natured, stress-free, common sense. Ann, herself a designer, cut Nicky's elaborate and beautifully handmade wedding dress herself.

The *chupah* was planned for three p.m. on Sunday afternoon on the grounds of the Sydney Yeshiva. Flowers (of course) were to be entwined around the poles of the *chupah*, and the florist had been booked to do the job at nine in the morning. On the Monday before the wedding, everything seemed ready and in place. Everyone knew what they had to do, and everything on the huge list was arranged and purring in anticipation of the day.

And then disaster struck.

On the Monday before the wedding it began to rain. It rained on Monday. It rained on Tuesday. It rained on Wednesday and Thursday.

*chapter 15*

The girls were beside themselves. What would happen to the dresses?! What would be with the mud?!

"I need you to do something for me right now," Ann said, clearly indicating that it wasn't negotiable.

"Go to Rabbi Feldman and send a fax to the Rebbe asking him to stop the rain!"

"Now who is crazy?" I gasped.

"I'm serious. Ask the Rebbe for a *brachah* that the weather will be fine for the wedding."

"Darling," I said kindly, "you can't be serious. The Rebbe is managing hundreds of thousands of important issues for so many people, and you want me to bother him with that?!"

"We are part of those people. Please, just do it for me. Go now!"

## SIX

And so I did. Rabbi Feldman was my conduit to the Rebbe at that time (through Rabbi Groner), and he was not at all censorious, despite my embarrassment over my task. I wrote the request in the name of my wife, and we faxed it late Thursday.

On Friday it rained again. On Shabbos it wasn't rain; it was a deluge. On Sunday morning, the girls all got up early for the makeup lady. It was raining. At about 11:30 in the morning the rain petered out, as though finally exhausted. Within an hour there was bright Sydney sunshine.

The whole wedding went beautifully and like clockwork.

It wasn't until we were all safely seated at the head table in the hall, each of our hearts differently flushed and bursting with pride and thanks to G-d for the *simchah*, that the rain resumed…

## SEVEN

A few days later, I received a call from Rabbi Feldman. He had been discussing some aspect of his work with Rabbi Groner, and he wanted to tell me about Rabbi Groner's final smiling question:

"By the way, how was the weather for the Kremnizer wedding?"

# The Note

*chapter 16*

One of my sons-in-law, Dovid, did not begin in Chabad. Although from a religious home, he came to Lubavitch through a series of degrees and choices.

As a schoolboy, he went to *yeshiva* after school, where he was inevitably influenced by Chabad, because that was the ethos of the Sydney Yeshiva.

After graduating high school, Dovid went to Yeshivah Gedolah in Melbourne, where he stayed for two years. Again, the very pronounced Chabad commitment there did its work, and although not yet entirely connected, he was on the way to becoming a fully committed Chasid. The Chabad influence in Yeshiva Gedola came from the teachers, of course, but it also came from the student *shluchim* (students

## Australian Encounters

sent by the Rebbe to study while serving as role models for the Australian boys).

When he was seventeen, his parents decided to take a world trip with their only son. Dovid's mother, a twin, was from a very holy lineage. Her twin sister was married to a Rebbe in New York, and she had other illustrious family in Israel. The plan was to take some time and visit these and other relatives in Israel and New York as well as some family graves.

Israel came first and then New York, where they stayed in Borough Park—the home of the US relatives.

After a few days, one of Dovid's uncles asked why Dovid had not yet been to Crown Heights. To assist, he asked his son, Dovid's cousin, to take him. During their visit, walking up one of the streets, they bumped into one of the *shluchim* who had befriended Dovid in Yeshiva Gedola. They embraced happily with the pleasure of seeing good friends in foreign geography. After chatting, bringing each other up to date on what they were each doing, and, more specifically, doing there, the *shliach* asked Dovid when he was going home. When Dovid replied, the *shliach* suggested that Dovid write to the Rebbe for a *brachah* for a safe journey.

Dovid is modest, and he felt that his connection to the Rebbe was not yet complete enough for him to write in—something he later regretted and of course rectified. Meanwhile, though, too shy to write personally, he asked the *shliach* to do so on his behalf.

*chapter 16*

When Dovid reminisces over what happened next, it is with the unjustified lament that he was such a baby then. As he was asking the *shliach* to write for him, the only thought that came into his mind was the story of the native dollars. Apparently, so Dovid had heard, when the Rebbe wanted to indicate a private connection to a person, he would give, together with his *brachah,* a dollar in the person's own home currency. As he was asking the *shliach* to write in for him, he secretly wished that the Rebbe would notice him enough to give him an Australian dollar.

A few days later, Dovid, having loved Crown Heights, decided to return there. As he was walking, he again bumped into the same *shliach*! Not only that, but the *shliach* announced triumphantly that he had written in for Dovid and the Rebbe had given his *brachah*.

The *shliach* then declared that the Rebbe had also instructed that he give Dovid *this.*

Dovid's blood ran cold. In disbelief, he stared at the *shliach's* outstretched hand. In it was a crisp, new, Australian dollar bill.

# I Just Need You to Arrange This for Me

*chapter 17*

### ONE

The year was 1980, and we were fully observant by then. I say this because as anyone who is observant will testify, this makes vacations difficult. Of course, there are resorts that cater for people who keep kosher, but in 1980 Australia, no such thing existed. This contributed to our accepting an invitation from some friends. A couple with whom we spent pleasant time together suggested that our two families holiday at a mountain retreat on the assurance that they would take care of all the (tedious) arrangements. Food, wine for Shabbat, vessels to eat from, and all peripheral issues were usually an inhibiting factor to go to a hotel (instead of a rented apartment), but in this case our friend, Sarah, promised that she would gladly make all the arrangements. All we had to do was turn up and pay our share. The children would love it, she pointed out, because there was a plethora of things for them to do, and that would allow the parents to have rest and recreation time.

The place they suggested was an interesting choice. It was a ski resort, but we were to go mid-summer. The mountain would be nearly empty, they explained, but the hotel was nice with good amenities for the children and good tennis courts for the husbands (we both played). The air was crisp and clean, and the surrounding meadows were safe for the children to run in. There were also pony rides, a swimming pool, and organized games for children.

We agreed and made the necessary arrangements. The place was about a six-hour drive from Sydney, and we arranged to set out at about the same time so the children could swap cars and seating to make the drive easier. At that time we had two daughters.

## TWO

My wife, Ann, had very difficult pregnancies. Both our children were born very premature and needed confinement in an incubator for some time. Apart from the (natural) anxiety this caused, Ann had other issues that caused suffering during pregnancy. She had bouts of kidney stone attacks, as well as other health disorders manifested in—and exacerbated by—pregnancy. Notwithstanding this, she remained

*chapter 17*

cheerful and optimistic throughout her confinements, as indeed she always was (and is) outside pregnancy.

## THREE

I was surprised at her silence during the drive. About four hours into the journey, when the children had returned to our car, our girls were fast asleep in the back of the car. Ann was uncharacteristically subdued, so I assumed that she was tired from the drive. I was completely unprepared for the shock that followed.

I heard an unfamiliar sound and looked over to find Ann's shoulders shaking while she sobbed in near silence. Shocked, I asked what was wrong. She couldn't speak. She just kept crying and shaking her head slowly. I decelerated to stop, but Ann motioned for me to continue.

Then her story slowly unfolded: Pregnancy was torture for her, consisting as it did of the birth of premature babies and the resultant psychological anguish, not to mention the traumatic health issues. And now she was pregnant again.

Pregnant! And what a way to find out! I wanted to celebrate, but obviously that was impossible, because Ann clearly needed comforting. I didn't have much time to wrestle with the ambivalence, however, because Ann cleared her throat and sternly (for her) required my silence and concentration while she told me something. This was made all the more dramatic in its incongruity from someone so usually easygoing. Half whispering so as not to wake the children, and without looking at me, she gave me what must have been some sort of prepared speech.

She pointed out that in addition to being married, we were also best friends. Accordingly, she expected me to show the extent of my commitment to her now. She couldn't possibly endure another pregnancy, let alone another birth. She needed me to take over, arrange an abortion, and do it in such a way that no one would know. She was particularly concerned that her parents and my mother never find out. She felt sick with guilt, but she simply couldn't face the prospect. She needed me to marshal my resources and fix it with the minimum of fuss and total secrecy—and, most importantly, she asked that I not try to dissuade her. I had to promise, she continued, not to add to her guilt and misery by trying to talk her out of it; rather, I should just accept her needs and fulfill them. She paused, took a deep breath, and said, "I just need you to arrange this for me."

## FOUR

As you can imagine, I was in silent turmoil. After assuring her that I would do whatever she needed, I tried to comfort her with soothing platitudes.

That done, and seeing her brighten up to a small degree, I was conscious of the girls in the back waking up and demanding her attention. This gave me time and space to think. What a roller coaster of emotion! On the one hand, Ann was pregnant, and we had a chance at a son! On the other hand,

*chapter 17*

I was convinced that she was telling the truth and that my poor darling just couldn't do it. What to do? How to manage this? I decided that since we were on holiday for ten days, there was nothing I could do immediately, so there was the welcome benefit of a breathing space. I would think much more, but not now. I tuned into helping Ann play "I spy" with our demanding treasures in the back.

### FIVE

The hotel was nice, if not great; it had large rooms and spaces and was generally comfortable. We had interconnecting rooms with the children, and there was a bathtub in their bathroom, so everyone was satisfied. Incredibly, looking back from the twenty-first century, the rooms did not have telephones! There were six public phones in the reception area, and they were the sole method of connecting with the outside world.

We settled in quickly, and the children were happy and busy. Our friends had not picked up on Ann's low spirits yet, because our interaction was still new enough for her to be able to conceal it. In private time, however, I could see how deeply sad she was with the whole situation. Poor Ann was conflicted with the natural desire for more children, the knowledge that she couldn't handle it, and the guilt and misery of that reality.

I had an idea.

I had a teacher, Rabbi Lesches, who happened to be in

## Australian Encounters

New York at the time. I could ring him and ask him to go to the Rebbe to ask for a *brachah*.

But how to manage it? Our day is their night and vice versa. I knew from past experience that if I wanted to speak to Rabbi Lesches while he was there, about lunchtime in New York was best. The problem was that one in the afternoon there was three in the morning at our hotel—with no phone in the room!

I believed it was important for Ann to feel she had my support, and if she woke up to find me gone at three a.m., she would guess what I was doing.

Nevertheless, that night I managed to stay awake, and when I was certain that everyone was asleep, I cautiously levered myself out of bed and tiptoed to the corridor. I rushed the considerable distance to reception, placed the call to New York, and was lucky enough to find Rabbi Lesches at the home of his in-laws (where he stayed when visiting New York). I told him the whole story and asked him to take a note to the Rebbe asking for a *brachah*. Characteristically, he was loudly upbeat, telling me he had heard that the Rebbe would be giving out dollars later that day. He then invited me to ring him back the next day at the same time.

I rushed back to the room, opened the door so slowly that it felt like an eternity, tiptoed to the bed, and slowly inserted myself back into bed. I held my breath for a few seconds and then slowly checked on Ann. Breathing steadily, she was fast asleep. So far, so good.

*chapter 17*

The next night, I found that it was easier to stay awake because of anxious anticipation. At 3:00 I repeated the previous night's exercise, just as delicately. When I got through to Rabbi Lesches, he was almost yelling in jubilation. He repeated what he had said to the Rebbe and shouted the Rebbe's response, which was that we had the *brachah*!

I returned to bed as vigilantly as the night before and remained awake for some time. What would happen? Should I tell Ann what I had done? Would that make a difference to her?

I need not have overthought the situation. I will never forget what happened in the morning, because it was one the most incredible moments of my life. Ann, depressed, guilt-ridden, and constantly near tears for the past few days, woke up and stretched. She then looked at me and announced with a smile that, on balance, maybe she could do this! After all, perhaps it would be a boy; we wanted a boy, and anyway it might be an easier pregnancy. In fact, she had just decided that she was going ahead. She told me to forget everything she had told me in the car; she would manage.

I remember standing there with my mouth open, dumbstruck. Fortunately, not noticing, she turned her now cheerful attention to the children.

It is spine-chilling to watch a miracle happen, suddenly completely changing a reality.

Needless to say, Ann managed the pregnancy, birth, and

# Australian Encounters

premature care marvelously, and with her customary cheerful optimism.

Today, our son is married, and he and his wife are parents of beautiful daughters of their own.

And our son has a younger sister…